PRAISE for B

MW00768136

"Buy this book before you start buying for your baby. A consumer's report for parents."
— Jack Bierman, Editor-In-Chief, L.A. PARENT, PARENTING and SAN DIEGO PARENT magazines

"As I read Ms. Silver's book, it occurred to me how absolutely invaluable it would have been to me when my daughter was a baby. Our staff found *BABY'S BEST!* incredibly comprehensive —everything parents need to know when shopping for baby clothes, toys, books and equipment."
— Liz White, Publisher of ATLANTA PARENT NEWSPAPER and ATLANTA BABY MAGAZINE

"A bundle of information! Baby products, 800 numbers, and resources—all at your fingertips."
— Lynn Varacalli, Editor, AMERICAN WOMAN MAGAZINE

"*BABY'S BEST!* is a must-have for any expecting or new parent. It's a time-, money- and effort-saver. Susan Silver has done the research and testing so new parents don't have to. The book is great!"
— Gwin Grogan, Managing Editor, DALLAS CHILD, AUSTIN CHILD and FORT WORTH CHILD magazines

"Reading *BABY'S BEST!* is like hearing advice from a good friend about which products she found most useful and enjoyable for her family. Very personal and encouraging with tidbits of motherly wisdom, yet highly professional and thoroughly researched. A must-read for new and expectant parents!"
— Ilana Hoffman, Managing Editor, PORTLAND PARENT NEWSMAGAZINE

more...

more...

"A carefully considered and solid guide to some excellent products that will ease the way for new-born parents. The book's an easy, pleasant read."
—Diana Huss Green, Editor-In-Chief, PARENTS' CHOICE MAGAZINE

"Definitely *BABY'S BEST!* An invaluable source for shopping for baby. Also includes helpful tips by author/mom Susan Silver."
—Donna Jefferson, Publisher, CHESAPEAKE CHILDREN NEWSPAPER (Maryland)

"*Be on the lookout for BABY'S BEST!* Author Susan Silver enables new parents to make informed decisions on the dizzying selection of the latest baby products. As a writer of parenting and family issues—and mother of two young children—I thought I had seen everything. Reading this book, I found myself taking notes for my own next time."
—Dianne R. McCann, Writer, BALTIMORE'S CHILD

"Especially valuable to new parents hungry for knowledge about products that will keep baby safe, comfortable and engaged."
—Sharon Sexton, Publisher, PARENTS EXPRESS (Philadelphia)

"This impressive guide will surely make life easier for the mother-to-be and all who love her! Current, comprehensive and full of common sense ideas. It's a catalogue, a resource book, and a reference for busy parents."
—Deborah Zink Roffino, Book Editor, SOUTH FLORIDA PARENTING

"This book would make a great shower gift for parents-to-be. It not only tells the readers what products are available, but also how much they cost and *where shoppers can find them!*"
—Dawn Lassiter, Media Reviewer, VALLEYKIDS PARENTING MAGAZINE (Illinois)

more...

"Susan Silver has done all the legwork (and saves new parents countless hours) by providing a great list of products for babies. This book is on my must-give list for all new parents...and grandparents!"
— Nancy Walter, Publisher, FAMILY TIMES (Wisconsin)

"Here's a book that is both useful and comprehensive. A consumer guide for parents, which will save them time and money. *BABY'S BEST!* will do away with the parenting dilemma buyer's hindsight."
— Pamila D. Kesterson, Publisher, THAT'S MY BABY MAGAZINE (Oregon)

"BABY'S BEST" is great even the second time around. As I prepare for my next arrival with less time now than ever before, I have found Susan's book to be especially helpful."
— Sharon Baumgold, attorney and mother of toddler and infant by the time this book comes out

Also by Susan Silver

ORGANIZED TO BE THE BEST! New Timesaving Ways to Simplify and Improve How You Work

The Best Baby (and Toddler) Products
to Make a Parent's Life Easier
and More Fun

Susan Silver

Adams-Hall Publishing
Los Angeles

Requests for such permissions should be addressed to:

Adams-Hall Publishing
PO Box 491002
Los Angeles, CA 90049

No patent liability is assumed with respect to the use of the information contained herein. While every precaution has been taken in the preparation of this book, the publisher and the author assume no responsibility for errors or omissions. Neither is any liability assumed for damages resulting from the use of the information contained herein.

Library of Congress Cataloging-in-Publication Data

Silver, Susan
    Baby's best!: the best baby (and toddler) products to make a parent's life easier and more fun / Susan Silver.
        p.   cm.
    Includes bibliographical references and index.
    ISBN 0-944708-33-1 (pbk.) : $9.95
    1. Infants' supplies--United States--Directories   I. Title.
RJ61.S6325 1993
649'.122'0296--dc20   93-16579
                                                                    CIP

Cover Design by Hespenheide Design (805/373-7336)
Front cover photograph: ©1989 Joan Hix Vanderschuit/Photobank, Inc.
Back cover photograph: Neil Ricklen (310/652-7651)

Adams-Hall books are available at special, quantity discounts for bulk purchases for sales promotions, premiums, fund-raising or educational use. For details, contact:

Special Sales Director
Adams-Hall Publishing
PO Box 491002
Los Angeles, CA 90049
1/800-888-4452

Printed in the United States of America
20 19 18 17 16 15 14 13 12 11 10 9 8 7 6 5 4 3 2 1
First printing 1993
First Edition   Printed on recycled paper

To expectant and experienced parents—may your parenting adventure be easier and more fun as well as richly rewarding.

Acknowledgments

Originally, *Baby's Best!* was supposed to be a 96-page book with 100 pictures. It ended up being a 224-page book with 224 photos and illustrations. Such an expansion was made possible by the contributions of many people, to whom I owe a debt of gratitude, professionally and personally.

Let me begin by thanking the experts I consulted who made time in their busy schedules to review part or all of the manuscript. My deepest appreciation goes to pediatric nurse practitioner Kittie Frantz, R.N, C.P.N.P; pediatrician James Varga, M.D., F.A.A.P.; pediatrician Ronald P. Becker, M.D.; dentist Sadie Mestman, D.M.D; certified lactation consultant Louise Tellalian, R.N., ASPO/Lamaze certified childbirth educator; Lynn Reed, R.N.; Debbie Albert, Executive Director of Juvenile Products Manufacturers Association; and Stephanie Tombrello, Executive Director of SafetyBeltSafe U.S.A.

I appreciate the many parenting publishers, editors and writers who took time to read the "advance proof" my publisher sent them and the wonderful comments they wrote, which appear on the back cover and the inside front pages.

Not all authors have the opportunity to get involved with book production but I fortunately have a publisher who encourages me to do so. It has been my special pleasure to work

xi

closely with several talented individuals during book production. Book designer Gary Hespenheide of Hespenheide Design, did a fantastic job on the front and back cover and the interior design elements. I was delighted to have the back cover photo taken by photographer Neil Ricklen, whose Simon & Schuster board books are featured in *Baby's Best!* Designer and production artist Junichi Hirota has an eye for detail and quality.

I remain grateful for the ongoing professionalism and perseverance displayed by Adams-Hall Publishing and their distributor, Publishers Group West.

I appreciate all of the firms who supplied background information, photographs or line art for the book. I especially appreciate the following individuals who provided special assistance to me: Bob Botts, Mary Kay Smith, Jan Stephens, Eliza Hunziker, Jakki Liberman, Shelly DiMattio, Sy Gershberg, Suzanne Mitchell, Jane Edwards, Karen Langevin, David Zapcic, Jack Martin, Mike Mand, Lise Wilks, Leslie Mapes, Anita Roewer, Cheryl Neverman, Christel Henke, Julie Rassel, Leslie Lucas, Stan Fridstein, Audie Fridstein, Annette McCullough and Helen McClary.

I've spent a lot of time at the office working on *Baby's Best!* and there are several people that have made it easier. Thanks go to Bruce, the UPS man, who cheerfully has handled an extra load of work; Harry, Larry and Greg, the 24-hour guards in my office building; and good friends Linda and Stan, who work in the building, for letting me use their heavy-duty xerox machine and for providing ongoing encouragement and friendship. I gratefully acknowledge the outstanding child care that Gail, Carmen and Jeannie have provided for my son, Charlie.

Thank you to my dear parents, mother-in-law, family and friends, whose support gives me balance and perspective.

Finally, this book wouldn't have been possible without my two loved ones—my husband, Don, and my son, Charlie. Besides being a loving husband and father, Don is himself a published author, whose editing and computer expertise were absolutely invaluable.

As for Charlie, he is the joy of my life. I can't wait to spend more time with him.

Contents

A "Read-Me-First" Introduction   xv

1   Newborn's Best   1

2   Nursing at Its Best   18

3   The Best Bottles and Accessories   25

4   The Best Mealtime Mates   31

5   The Best Bath   40

6   Indoors at Its Best   50

7   The Best On-the-Go Products   64

8   The Best Dressed Baby   81

9   The Best Toys for Babies   89

10   The Best Toys for Toddlers   103

11   The Best Tapes and Books   119

12   The Best Resources for Parents   134

Baby's Best! Gift Guide   145

Appendix: How to Contact Companies and Organizations Featured in Baby's Best!   160

About the Author   179

A Personal Note From the Author and Charlie   181

Index   183

A
"Read-Me-First"
Introduction

Please don't skip this introduction. You'll need it to discover the fastest, most efficient way for you to use this book because first and foremost, this book is designed to help save you time. And with a baby or toddler you're going to need to save time as you've never done before in your entire life.

I should know. As a nationally recognized organization expert who had her first baby one and a half years ago, I've seen what can happen even when you're already organized. What most amazed me is how much time I've spent just taking care of the daily needs of my baby son (who's now my 1½-year-old toddler). I marvel at how his needs have changed so rapidly and how much time I've spent just *shopping* for him. Hopefully, you'll do considerable shopping before your baby arrives (but I do understand the superstitious fear of doing too much preparation for a baby who hasn't yet been born.) Whenever you shop, you should use this book as a shopping guide *to save you time and money* because it's an overwhelming marketplace out there where it's hard to find just what you really need and will use.

HOW THIS BOOK WILL HELP YOU
To save you time, I have provided a select number of products with very specific product information that includes brand names,

model numbers, suggested retail prices and 800 numbers to call. I have either used, tested or reviewed products firsthand or have done enough research and comparison shopping to recommend a product as something I would buy and use the "next time" I have a baby. Since "a picture is worth a thousand words," and therefore, an instant time-saver, I've included more than 220 of them. It's impossible to find this kind of specific, select up-to-date product information between the covers of a book, until now.

Besides saving you time and money, I intend to help save you energy so you can put it where it's needed most, with your baby. Besides wasting your energy on shopping, it's also easy to waste it on products that don't work.

Products should offer solutions, not more problems. I get very excited about quality, innovative products and companies that are actually improving the quality of parents' lives.

A reporter from The Wall Street Journal (who was not a parent) asked me an interesting question about the products in my book, "Are these products really necessary?" If necessity is the mother of invention, then motherhood and fatherhood have their fair share of necessity, which demands inventive, innovative products.

As a parent, an organization consultant and an author, I love to share information about good products. I will be pleased if even one product in this book either saves you from the brink of total exhaustion or lifts you beyond your expectations to sheer exhilaration so that the door to your child has opened a little wider. I will be happy if you discover a half dozen or more products that make a difference. I'll be thrilled if dozens make parenting easier and more fun for you.

By "easier," I mean several things. You'll of course be saving time and energy. But you'll "breathe easier" because you'll be using quality products that are beneficial and safe for your baby and toddler.

Because parenting is the hardest job in the world, I hope that some of these products help you have more "fun" with your baby, too. Both you and your baby deserve that, as well as having the "best" products for you both. "Best," by the way, doesn't refer to the most costly or the most fashionable or trendy. For me, the best products are highly functional and reflect the criteria I've listed below in the next section.

I take the responsibility of sharing product information seriously. I represent no companies in this book and will do my utmost to point out a down side to a product, when necessary.

I'll also be sharing my experiences and from time to time, I'll even give some motherly advice or special organization tips or ways I've used the products.

Finally, I'm very excited to provide the special *Baby's Best!* **Gift Guide** on pages 145-59 that lists selected products in this book by category and by price (and of course, has page reference numbers). This guide will help you quickly pinpoint baby and toddler gift suggestions whether you're a parent, expectant parent, grandparent, aunt, uncle, cousin or friend.

HOW I SELECTED THE BEST PRODUCTS

I began with a basic core of quality products that I and my husband, Don, had used with our son, Charlie. I contacted the manufacturers or distributors of those products and discovered others to review or test.

I also attended the most recent Juvenile Products Manufacturers Association trade show and discovered the latest products as well as prototypes for those to be introduced in the future. I've combed dozens of product catalogs, mail order catalogs and parenting magazines and newspapers. I consulted with experts in specialized areas, such as breastfeeding, dentistry, car passenger safety and consumer product education. Friends who are parents also shared their special favorites, too. I've tested or examined countless samples.

I don't wish to suggest, however, I've seen everything. And for products I've missed, please contact me (see page 181 for a quick and easy way). I intend to do updated editions (as I've done with my first book, *ORGANIZED TO BE THE BEST! New Timesaving Ways to Simplify and Improve How You Work*).

I had a number of criteria for selecting "the best" products. I looked for quality, safe products that were special, innovative or highly functional. I included some products because they were versatile, had multiple uses or could be used for a long period of time, past the first three years (which is roughly the time frame I'm using for this book).

I looked for products (and companies) that are ecology conscious and more naturally oriented.

Whenever possible, I looked for pioneering companies and products that had really developed a new idea or innovation. I tried to avoid knock-off products (but sometimes it's difficult to tell).

I asked *where* products are made. My preference is U.S.-made goods as I want to support quality American companies. When I began the book, I had had my own boycott of all goods made in China because I was aware of a problem concerning the exploitation of prison labor by some companies. I took a lot of extra time asking questions of every company who has products made there (and the majority of the companies in the book do). I received satisfactory answers confirming that non-prison labor was manufacturing products and that most companies have representatives who regularly inspect manufacturing operations in China.

I asked about any special awards, recognition or publicity a product had received. In general, I was more impressed with formal awards or certification programs such as those offered by the Juvenile Products Manufacturers Association (JPMA), *Parents' Choice*, *Oppenheim Toy Portfolio* and The National Parenting Center (see pages 140, 136, 136-37 and 142 respectively).

I also asked companies about any recalls for products being considered for this book (two companies openly discussed two voluntary recalls and the other companies said no recalls had taken place).

I looked for products that offered value to the consumer and reflected my own values and the features I most wanted to see. The price of a product was not a major factor, which is not to say that the sky was the limit. Many of the products turned out to be quite inexpensive. But when I look at value, I'm looking at what a product can offer. If a product offers one or more important solutions for a parent, the cost in dollars and cents may not be a main factor, at least for me.

Products that are easy to use are particularly important to myself and my husband as we are both "mechanically disabled." I'm willing to read a manual but if I have to start drilling holes and using hardware, I quickly lose my enthusiasm for a product.

This book is a very personal approach to product selection. These are *my* criteria and as you read, you'll see more of what I looked for in any given product or product area. They may not reflect all of *your* criteria, but at least you will know where I stand and just *why* I made product selections. If you agree or disagree, let me know. I'd love to hear from you and so would Charlie (see A Personal Note From the Author and Charlie on page 181).

HOW TO BEST USE THIS BOOK

My aim is to make using this book as quick and easy for you as possible, whether you're a parent, an expectant parent or someone looking for baby gifts.

If you're a new or expectant parent, you probably won't be reading the entire book straight through. You should start by going to the table of contents on page xiii to see which are the most critical chapters to read right now. The opening paragraph or two of each chapter will give you a quick summary of what you'll find in a chapter.

The detailed index lists products, trade names, companies and organizations that are organized and cross referenced for your convenience. The index will come in handy whether you're looking for a type of product (for example, "bottles"), a specific brand name product ("POPUPS") or a company ("Prince Lionheart"). The index will let you look up information in a variety of ways, very quickly and easily.

Within the text, you'll find cross referencing with specific page numbers to minimize going to the index to look up page numbers.

Within every chapter you'll find specific product availability or how-to-order information for each product and in most cases, a toll-free 800 number in bold type for the manufacturer or distributor. If a company has several products in the same chapter, there will be a product availability cross reference back to the first page that the company appeared in the chapter. If there are several products from the same company, the availability information will appear either with the first product that's mentioned or at the end of the last product.

Close to the 800 number you'll see a state in parentheses to help you better gauge a time zone. It's probably best to make calls between 9:00 a.m and 4:00 p.m in any particular time zone. Of course, some major companies have longer, extended hours to accommodate the different time zones nationwide. I've also converted all those clever phone numbers that spell out words (and take forever to dial) back to easy-to-dial digits. If an 800 number is busy or if you live somewhere that doesn't let you use the 800 number, use the appendix, which starts on page 160, to find alternate phone numbers as well as addresses.

When you see the words *"Be on the lookout for"* be alerted to new, promising products I discovered through my research that weren't yet available for me to review. When you see the words

xx   *BABY'S BEST!*

"Next time," know that this is definitely a product I would want to buy and use the next time I have a baby.

I have used the trademark symbols, ® and ™, usually just the first time a trademarked product is mentioned in a chapter to avoid interfering with the flow of the text.

Finally, use this book whenever you shop for baby products and be sure to use the "Shopping Notes" pages at the end of the book to keep all of your product information organized in one place.

A FEW IMPORTANT CONSUMER TIPS

Become a reader. Read the entire box or packaging thoroughly before you buy or open anything. Read all warnings and suggestions.

Read the "suggested ages" but keep in mind they may be safety related rather than age appropriate (see pages 89-90), may be exaggerated in order to sell more product or may simply not be suitable for your baby or toddler.

Read the manual and follow instructions carefully. Set aside quiet time when you won't be interrupted.

Read the laundry tags and don't cut them out unless, of course, they are irritating your baby. It's so frustrating when you get a wonderful hand-me down garment and find the laundry label has been removed. Most quality items will be passed on to other children.

Because prices are "suggested retail prices" that vary considerably between different stores and states, I have used the term "about" before most prices, which are usually rounded off. In some cases a price range is given. In rare cases, I couldn't obtain a price from a company. (Prices don't include tax or shipping.)

As for trying to locate a specific product in a store, here are a few suggestions. *Always call the store first* to check for availability of an item and if possible, have it pulled for you and put at the main desk. If the store is a big, discount store that won't do that, ask for the exact aisle number.

If a store is out of stock or doesn't carry that particular item, ask if they can order it for you and how long it will take. If it will take too long or the store can't do a special order, ask for other stores they recommend trying and say you will mention their store name when referred.

Also try calling the phone number for the company that makes the product. Be aware, however, that often a company can only tell you where their products *in general* are carried, not which stores carry specific products. Sometimes, however, a company is willing to take direct orders and that information is usually noted in the book. Be sure to call a company if you've had great difficulty locating one of their products; the company may be able to accommodate you even if they don't normally sell directly to the consumer.

Often it's just easier to order by phone or mail, especially for those products in this book that have direct mail sources. You may pay a little extra with the shipping charge, but think of what your time is worth making all those phone calls and driving in your car plus paying for the gas. A few extra dollars may well be worth it. Almost all direct mail sources included in *Baby's Best!* accept credit cards.

Let's talk about the big, discount, mass merchant stores versus the independents. I like them both. Sure, it's fun to get a better price or deal. But be aware, that the independents or smaller retailers may offer you some real advantages.

First, you may get better service, more personalized in-store or on-the-phone help. Second, they may be able to special order one item for you that a larger store wouldn't bother with. Third, they may also have a selection of specialty items that are impossible to find in mass merchandise stores.

If we don't buy from local smaller retailers, they will simply disappear and no longer be an option for consumers in the marketplace. Both product selection and service will go down. You'll then have to wait longer for items that may only be available through the mail.

Please don't shop by price alone. There are many costs that go into shopping for and buying merchandise. Look at all the hidden costs of your time, phone charges and gas expenditures. Consider, too, the extra service, convenience or expertise a company or catalog may be offering to make it well worth paying a little more.

If you like getting products right away but dislike having to drive to a local retailer, ask if they'll ship it to you through UPS (United Parcel Service). For a few extra dollars you can get a product right away and save yourself time and trouble. (UPS usually provides next day delivery in the same city or vicinity at their lowest rate.)

Here's a time and money saver that's also good for the environment: buy rechargeable batteries and a recharging unit. Our system is made by GE and should be available at a hardware or large drug store, where we bought ours. Between all the products and toys you'll accumulate, you could go through many batteries. In the long run you'll save both time and money recharging your own batteries and do a good turn for the environment, too.

1

Newborn's Best

Some expectant parents really get swept up in the excitement and anticipation of a new baby and eagerly set up and decorate their nursery. Others take a more wait-and-see-what-we'll-need approach. My husband Don and I took this approach.

While we became very committed to our Lamaze techniques and the anticipated (or should I say dreaded?) birth process, frankly, it was hard, for me anyway, to picture having a real baby and all that being a parent entailed—including the preparation of the nursery. We were fortunate to have many friends and family members who loaned or gave us many things. But there were so many other products I was to discover for the nursery and looking back, wished I had known about *before* Charlie was born.

SLEEPING LIKE A BABY
Although I had a crib right away for my infant, Charlie, I didn't use it for him during the first couple of months. I preferred using the movable wicker bassinet on wheels and the wooden cradle that our friends Elaine and Leo had loaned to us. A bassinet or cradle provides a nicer, cozier, more womb-like environment than a big crib and fits more conveniently in different rooms of your home. *No matter where your baby sleeps,*

1

check with your pediatrician for a recommended sleeping position.
We kept the bassinet mainly in the living room for Charlie's naps and the cradle remained beside our bed at night (which made nighttime nursings very convenient). If you live in a two-story home, having either a bassinet or cradle downstairs is a must.

Next time (especially if Charlie's little brother or sister were another moderate-to-high-demand baby) I would want to have the **Soothe 'n Snooze Bassinet** (about $169) by New Age Concepts to provide an even more comfortable, womb-like environment that studies show helps settle babies, especially those who have difficulty going to sleep. The size and shape of a bassinet, the Soothe 'n Snooze has a patented orbital motion that replicates the movement a baby feels in the womb. The sound of the motor also provides a white background noise that may also be comforting. New Age Concepts spent four years researching, designing, developing and testing this product. Test results on 38 babies included the following: 79 percent reported their babies had fewer nights in which they experienced difficulty sleeping, 61 percent reported their babies woke up fewer times during the night while using the Soothe 'n Snooze and 48 percent reported their babies took less time to fall asleep while using it. Call New Age Concepts (California) at **800/477-8009** for stores that carry this product.

If you don't need all the special womb effects and you want a practical, portable and pretty bassinet, consider the **Fisher-Price® Gentle Glide Bassinet** (about $100). This one's loaded with useful features and extras. You can glide it manually back and forth to soothe your baby. You can detach it from the stand for room-to-room portability or take it traveling by storing the legs in the base of the stand. It comes with an adjustable canopy, mattress pad, fitted sheet, bassinet liner and skirt. The liner and sheet are machine washable. Check availability of the bassinet at major retailers such as Toys R Us, Wal-Mart, K-Mart and Target or call Fisher-Price (New York) **800/432-KIDS** for stores near you.

If you decide not to use a bassinet or cradle for your baby and go straight to a crib because you don't want to buy equipment that you'll only use for a few months, there are some wonderful products I wish I had known about that can make your crib into a very cozy, comfortable place.

A natural lambskin is one such product. Medical studies have confirmed what Hippocrates noted back in 377 BC—that lambskin provides an excellent sleeping environment for young children. It is used extensively in hospitals in the U.S.A as well as in Canada, Australia and Europe.

The **Lamby Cuddle Rug** (about $60) is a natural, medical quality lambskin that helps your baby settle more quickly and sleep better. Charlie was about 13 months when I bought our Lamby. I'm confident that it helps him with his sleep (which isn't his strong suit!) but I wish I had been using this terrific product from day one.

For maximum tactile benefit, Charlie is on the fleece side of the Lamby without any sheet between the Lamby and him. In his earlier drooling days, I would have placed a cloth or the "Crib Bib" (see page 5) under his head on top of the lambskin to prevent soiling. You can use Lamby year round as it stays cool and dry in the summer (wool quickly absorbs and dissipates humidity and perspiration) and warm and cozy in the winter (it's a natural insulator).

Designed specifically for use with infants, Lamby has been specially clipped and tanned. It's safe, non-toxic and doesn't shed. Besides the crib, Lamby can be used in a cradle, stroller, or play yard and is great for traveling and visiting because of the comforting familiarity. It's machine washable but should be air dried.

I was relieved to learn, too, that Lamby lambs are not bred just for their skin. Lamby is a natural by-product of the lamb/sheep industry in Australia, just as leather goods are a natural by-product of the U.S. beef industry.

I bought my Lamby from the Bringing Up Baby catalog (California) at **310/826-5774**. You can also call Lamby Nursery Collection (Washington) at **800/669-0527** for a store near you.

The **Baby-Snuggleheads™** patented safety cushion ($23 to $32) is another product I would use in a crib to help an infant settle more quickly into a sleeping position. Proven effective in hospital nurseries, this product satisfies a baby's "back-to-the-womb" instinct of nestling. Ever since Charlie was a tiny infant, he has scooted up to the end of crib to nestle his head. When he was a newborn, my husband and I worried about it and often moved him away from the cradle rails and bumper pads.

The Baby-Snuggleheads cushion establishes safe sleeping

boundaries away from crib rails and bumpers, provides a stable and dependable pattern for slumber and according to the manufacturer, Rock-A-Bye Baby, reduces crying and fussing before sleep. It has a non-slip rubberized bottom and internal weights that keep it firmly in place. Baby-Snuggleheads cushions are machine washable and dryable, come in cotton or satin in full term or preemie sizes. You can order Baby-Snuggleheads by calling Rock-A-Bye Baby (Florida) at **800-ROCK-A-BYE (800/762-5229)** for the nearest retailer or ordering by phone through Baby Club of America (Connecticut) at **800/PLAYPEN (800/752-9736)**.

 Two other wonderful products by Rock-A-Bye Baby also are supposed to be helpful for settling your new baby. They are **Rock-A-Bye Bear®** (about $45) in two styles and **Rock-A-Bye Bunny®** (about $60). Beautifully designed and crafted of high quality material, these soft animals feature authentic intrauterine sounds, which were obtained by placing a special microphone inside a pregnant mother's womb directly next to the unborn infant's ear just prior to labor. The sounds have been placed on a computer chip inside a special audio unit in the product.

Since hospital studies have shown that recorded intrauterine sounds are soothing and calming to newborns, I would want one of these two products next time. When your baby sleeps, you get to sleep and that's worth a lot. The bear comes in two different color combinations: light brown and white or high contrast white and black with a red ribbon. The bunny is white and pastel plum. They are available by calling Rock-A-Bye Baby (Florida) at **800-ROCK-A-BYE (800/762-5229)** for the nearest retailer or ordering by phone through The Baby Club of America (Connecticut) at **800/PLAYPEN (800/752-9736)**.

I would also consider Ameda/Egnell's **Baby Calmer™** (No. R12364, about $30), which was developed by a physician and is used in hospitals worldwide. The pure "shhh" sound of the seashell-shaped Baby Calmer first attracts and then quiets fussy babies. According to Ameda/Egnell, 87 percent of all babies who hear the soothing sound will stop crying, calm themselves and often fall asleep, relaxing both parent and baby alike. It won't suppress cries for help and it shuts off automatically. It comes with a nine-volt battery. Call Ameda/Egnell (Illinois) **800/323-8750** for a local distributor or to order direct.

One crib product has a calming effect on anyone who has ever struggled with changing crib sheets. **Dreamsheet™ Quick Change Bedding** ($50 to $60) lets you change bedding in seconds without removing the bottom sheet and bumper. It comes with  a fitted bottom anchor sheet that stays on the mattress and two moisture-proof combination top sheet/mattress pads that attach easily with four, hook and loop, self-fastening tabs. The top sheets are reversible with a brushed, flannel-like tricot for cool weather and a polished, poly-cotton for warm weather. Both the bottom and top sheets are machine washable on a low temperature setting. The manufacturer ideally recommends that you air dry the top sheets (or machine dry them on low) but warns against using a medium or high temperature. Call Judi's Originals (Arizona) at **800/421-9433** for a dealer near you.

No matter what bedding you use, the Sandbox Industries **CRIB BIB®** (two to a package for $16 to $18) is an essential addition to prevent unnecessary linen changes. When Charlie was spitting up and drooling, he did it on the CRIB BIB, not the sheet. Made of a double thick reversible quilted cotton on one side and a soft terry on the other, the CRIB BIB prevents wetness from soaking through and saves frequent laundering of sheets. It measures 48 by 7 inches, ties onto crib bars and comes in 18 solid colors and several prints. It's available through Bellini and USA Baby stores throughout the U.S. or by mail order through The Right Start Catalog (California) at **800-548-8531** and One Step Ahead (Illinois) at **800/274-8440**.

As for **cribs**, I haven't been terribly impressed by what I've seen. I will share a few observations on what I'd look for in a crib today. First, look for JPMA certification (see page 140) or at least some reference to the safety standards set by CPSC (see pages 140-41). Second, look for a single-hand drop-side mechanism with a kick stand that works easily. Third, look for a four-position adjustable mattress support. Fourth, look for multi-use convertibility or extended use.

I'm anxious to examine the **Tabor Crib-n-Twin** (No. 280, about $649), which according to their literature, has all of these features. I especially like that the crib converts to both an intermediate toddler size bed and then to a twin bed, providing many years of continued use. There's a drawer under the crib (and later twin) bed, as well as three storage drawers (that later convert into a free-standing three-drawer night table). All drawers are on easy-glide rails and have stops. Call Tabor Designs/Desta Inc. (Florida) at **800/822-6748**.

If your baby ever sleeps or naps apart from you in another room, in the nursery, for example, buy a baby monitor. With a baby monitor, you can be in one room and through a receiving device, hear all the sounds in your baby's room, including breathing or crying. Next time I would buy the **Gerry Look 'N Listen Baby Monitor** (Model 604, about $40) because it has these important features: an alarm that goes off when the battery is low, an indicator light that tells you when the parent's receiving unit is out of range, a choice of two FM channels to improve reception, portability of both the transmitting and receiving units and a visual sound display. The range is 300 feet in open air but will vary greatly depending on the kinds of interference you have in your home. *Be on the lookout for* Gerry's two-way unit (Model 609) through which you can talk to your baby (but it won't be as powerful or have as great a range). It will, however, be a product that can grow with your family and be used in a variety of situations. Call Gerry (Colorado) at **800/525-2472** for a store in your area.

And when you're checking on your baby at night, it's nice to have a soft light. We have a dimmer on our overhead light. You might prefer instead the **Musical/Touch Lite Lamp** (about $75) by Judi's Originals, which I saw at the JPMA show (see page xi). This is a darling baby lamp with a wind-up music box that features a heart-shaped "touch" sensitive pad that lets parents use a standard 40 watt bulb and have the benefits of a three-way bulb that provides soft night light, medium light and full illumination. The lamp is decorated with one of several different charming characters, each of which coordinates with Judi's bedding ensembles. For availability, see Judi's Originals on page 5.

Pansy Ellen's **Crib Light** (Model 330, about $10) is a manual or voice activated light. If a baby fusses or cries during the night, a soothing light will activate for approximately five minutes—usually enough time for a baby to fall asleep. It's available in retail chains nationwide and you can call Pansy Ellen (Georgia) at **404/751-0442** for a local store. See also Pansy-Ellen's combination **CribEssentials Musical Mobile and Crib Light** on pages 90-91.

Finally, you will probably want to have a soft front carrier that you wear to hold your newborn baby (we used ours until Charlie was about five months, although some can be used longer). Charlie slept very well in the carrier as I wore it several times during the day. He also found it to be an ideal way to go to sleep; the only problem was he required a walking motion along with it. Sometimes it got to be rather tiresome to have to walk him to sleep, which usually took 30 to 45 minutes. Already suffering from sleep deprivation ourselves, my husband and I weren't always thrilled with what we called our "Feet-Don't-Fail-Me-Now-Routine" of getting Charlie to go to sleep. But frankly, I don't know what we would have done without our carrier (especially since I hadn't known then about the other calming devices described in this chapter).

The consensus is that babies find this way of being carried very comforting and many experts believe that an infant who is carried this way for several hours each day will cry less. The carrier we used was a hand-me-down. Its major drawback was a lack of an easy way to remove Charlie without waking him once he was asleep. We usually needed the deft skill of a bomb squad member trying to safely defuse an explosive device.

Next time I would probably get the patented, six-position baby carrier called the **Tot Tenders Baby Carrier** (about $47). The main advantage is that since the baby wears the baby section, it's easier to remove a sleeping baby from the carrier and not wake him. You can easily put the baby down to sleep or if you're running errands, can return a sleeping baby more easily to the car seat. It's easier to remove the baby from the carrier than to initially get the baby into the carrier. However, I'm reassured to know that this carrier was designed and tested by 100 new parent families over a seven-year period.

This versatile, quality, U.S.-handcrafted carrier can later be used as a back carrier, in a forward-facing position, as a restraining device in a shopping cart or as an emergency high chair on outings. There are padded shoulder straps, a pocket for necessities, a toy/pacifier strap and a removable, reversible bib to protect your clothing and your baby's face. A baby can nurse without your removing the carrier. Tot Tenders provides a helpful instruction sheet and also is happy to talk with consumers on their helpline. I first saw this product through the Bringing Up Baby catalog (California) at **310/826-5774** or you can order direct through Tot Tenders (Oregon) at **800/634-6870**.

IT'S CHANGING TIME AGAIN (AND AGAIN)

Since your baby will have undergone an estimated 3,000 plus diaper changes up to the age of two, you should give serious thought to the changing area(s) you set up.

I selected the **Bellini 3 Drawer Dressing Chest** (35 by 18 by 58 inches, in the Corso series, about $599), which is a combi-

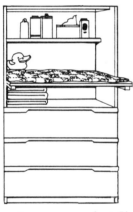

nation changing table and chest of drawers (the latter can be used for many years). Because this changing table is oversized and partially enclosed on three sides, it's much more difficult for a baby to roll off. (And of course, you'll always have at least one hand holding the baby at all times on any changing table.)

I also like this table because it allows me to change my baby, Charlie, in a more accessible position. Instead of side facing, as with most changing tables, he is front facing, with his head at the back panel of the changing table and his feet toward me. I can see what I'm doing more easily and hence, do a more thorough job. You also have more eye contact and interaction with your baby. The down side is you risk getting kicked occasionally as your baby grows but that's a risk I'm willing to take.

To make this changing table even safer, I removed the middle, modular mini-shelf, which hindered smoothly lifting Charlie up and off the table. I also have a small, firm pillow that serves as a softer "headrest" than the back panel. Next time I would use the **BUMP AROUND**™ ($30 to $37) by Sandbox™ Industries to protect my baby's head and make the changing table cozier and even more secure. Made of thick, quilted terry with rolled sides, it's machine washable and dryable, has a water repellent lining,

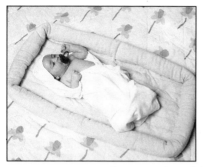

comes in nine colors and is made in the U.S. Besides on the changing table, it can be used after a bath on the bed or the floor as a portable changing pad. It comes in two sizes: Style 5000 is 17 by 34 inches and Style 5000M is 24 by 38 inches. Call Sandbox Industries (New Jersey) at **800/451-6636** to ask them for the name of a store near you that carries this product.

Back to Bellini, since I've only covered half the story. Below the changing table is a deep shelf space I use for storing diapers and below that are three drawers that are fairly deep, operate smoothly with metal glides and have internal stops so kids can't pull out the drawers. (Here are a couple of drawer organization tips: use shallow boxes without tops to separate different types of clothing and label the outside drawers using Post-it brand Removable Magic Tape and permanent markers such as the Sharpie brand. Press the tape labels securely in place right in front of the section of the drawer that contains a particular clothing item. For example, Charlie's top drawer has labels from left to right for "short-sleeved shirts," "long-sleeved shirts," "socks" and "sleepwear.") Labeling the drawers also makes it easy for fathers, grandparents and other caregivers to quickly find a desired item.

When Charlie is finally potty trained, the Bellini 3 Drawer Changing Chest will make a versatile transformation into a three-drawer chest with three shelves above it. The first shelf is the one I use now for diaper storage. The changing table conveniently slides back in to make a second shelf. (There's no changing table top to store.) I'll buy a third modular shelf (about $49) from Bellini that installs easily. To be sure, this piece of furniture isn't inexpensive, but considering the built-in quality and versatility for many years to come, I think it's well worth it.

There are many other companion pieces that you can add, too. The Corso series pieces come in white (which was my choice), natural and whitewash. All pieces are available exclusively through the more than 50 licensed Bellini outlets in the U.S.. Call Bellini (New Jersey) at **800/332-BABY (800/332-2229)** for your closest store.

I use several products that make my changing table area more convenient. The **Zojirushi Airpot** is a push button thermos I use to store fresh, warm water. I discovered this wonderful product after having read about keeping warm water in a "thermos with a pump" in Marianne Neifert's book  *Dr. Mom*. I called store after store and finally found the Zojirushi non-electric, thermal Airpot at a local store. Whenever possible, I prefer using natural water rather than baby wipes to clean Charlie. Neifert, who is an award-winning pediatrician and mother of five, indicates that wipes can be irritating and that warm water with a washcloth (we use a clean cloth diaper) works just as well.

The Airpot has superior insulation and keeps water warm for many, many hours. With a 73-year track record as a leader in advanced thermal technology design, Zojirushi invented the Airpot in 1973. I use model number AAB-22 (about $59) which features a handy see-through water level gauge that lets you see how much water you have left. It stores 2.2 liters (2.32 quarts) and comes in red or white (I have the white because it's more of a nursery color).

The AALB-19 is less expensive (about $34) but comes without the gauge and holds 1.85 liters (1.95 quarts). It's available in white or two delicate floral designs. Both models have swivel bases and will make great coffee servers later on. (Zojirushi cautions against using any milk products in the Airpot.) Call Zojirushi (California) at **800/733-6270** for a distributor near you.

For the times I do use wipes at the changing table, I use the **Comfy Wipe Warmer** by Rock-A-Bye Baby (about $24). You just  wrap the cover around a box of wipes, plug in the cord and baby's bottom is in heaven with warmed-up wipes, which normally are cool or cold to the touch. Babies can jump from this cool sensation (wouldn't you?) and this discomfort can contribute to increased hostility and resistance to diaper changing. A patented, wrap-around warmer with adjustable Velcro® straps that adapts to most sizes of wipes containers, it's UL approved and made in the U.S. The decorative quilted cover is machine washable and dryable. The warmer is available by calling Rock-A-Bye Baby (Florida) at **800-ROCK-A-BYE (800/762-5229)** for the nearest retailer or ordering by phone through The Baby Club of America (Connecticut) at **800/PLAYPEN (800/752-**

9736).

Speaking of wipes, I use the **NewDay's Choice Baby Wipes** because they have a gentle, all-natural formula and come in a special easy-to-use refill pack (about $2.50 for 84) that drops into any rectangular plastic tub. The refill uses almost 90 percent less plastic than a new tub, takes up far less landfill space and is more economical. In addition, these wipes aren't bleached with elemental chlorine, which can release harmful dioxins into the environment.

I recommend using organizers at the changing table. **THE ORGANIZER™** by Prince Lionheart (about $13) is a functional and convenient nursery organizer I use to store diapering sup-plies, toiletry articles and small toys. (You'll want to have toys at your changing table, especially when those little hands are better able to grasp and reach for all kinds of things, including the clean-up task itself.) The Organizer features four compartments, a swing-away carrying handle and a special hook-on hanger that lets you attach it to your changing table. Besides nursery items, this is also a handy organizer later on for stationery, sewing, cosmetic or toiletry items. Call Prince Lionheart at **800/544-1132** (805/922-2250 in California) for a local store or to mail order this item, which is made in the U.S.

If I didn't have a built-in space for diapers in my changing table, I'd want to have **The First Years Nursery Organizer** (No. 3111, about $9.60.) The center pocket holds about 16 diapers and the four see-through side pockets are great for diapering supplies and small toys. You can attach it to a changing table or wall. For store locations, call The First Years/Kiddie Products, Inc. (Massachusetts) at **800/533-6708**.

I like having a baby laundry bag hanging at the changing table. My favorite is the **Bumkins Waterproof Tote Bag** (about $9), a two-section drawstring bag made out of a unique, waterproof treated fabric that was originally developed for diaper products. It is durable and can endure many, many machine washings without losing its waterproof properties.

I use the large, elastic mesh front pocket to separate white clothes from colored. You could also use this pocket to separate dry, soiled clothes from wet ones. With its special combination drawstring/shoulder strap, this bag is also handy as a sandbox, beach or swim tote. It's sold through juvenile retail stores across the U.S. Call Bumkins (Arizona) at **602/254-2626** for your nearest store.

Other laundry bags to consider are washable drawstring mesh bags such as **The First Years Wash 'N Dry Bag** (No. 3105, about $2.10) and the **Safety 1st Wash'r Dry Bag** (No. 156, about $2.20). I saw a prototype of the new **Safety 1st Baby's Own Laundry Bag** (No. 252, about $6), which was a roomy 18 by 18 inches and included a zipper closure. For store locations, call The First Years/Kiddie Products, Inc. (Massachusetts) at **800/533-6708** and Safety 1st (Massachusetts) at **800/962-7233**.

As far as diapers are concerned, I use a combination of disposables (there's no brand I particularly recommend) and a cloth diaper service. Besides being ecologically superior in my opinion, cloth diapers are great for cleanups at the changing table and with a service, I don't have to launder them!

I'm anxious to test two new cloth diaper products: **Ecology Kids™ Changing Time™ Diaper Cover** and their **Super Absorbent Diaper**. Both products feature a special breathable, waterproof outer covering that changes color and reads "CHANGE ME" when a baby is wet or soiled. (It's the heat that creates the change, not the wetness). The Super Absorbent Diaper is an "all-in-one" diaper that features not only this outer covering but also an attached, super absorbent pad constructed of six fabric layers, with a special fiber blend (created by DuPont Company) that helps draw moisture away from your baby's skin. Both the Diaper Cover and the Super Absorbent Diaper come in newborn, medium, large and extra-large sizes. You can call Diplomat Juvenile Corp., the maker of the Ecology Kids line, located in New York, at **800/247-9063** for a store near you.

As for diaper pails, I really like the **Fisher-Price® Diaper Pail** (No. 9116, about $18) we use, which has a  handy foot pedal that leaves hands free and a securely locking lid. It has a hidden deodorizer compartment and a special inner lid with two swinging panels that allow a diaper to drop through easily. The lid is also an odor barrier and holds a plastic liner in place. Major retailers such as Toys R Us, Wal-Mart, K-Mart and Target carry the Fisher-Price brand or call Fisher-Price (New York) at **800/432-KIDS (800/432-5437)** for stores.

MAKING THE MOST
OF THOSE PRECIOUS WAKEFUL MOMENTS

I was surprised to discover how much I enjoyed changing time when Charlie was a newborn. It's not that I enjoyed dirty diapers (who does?!) but rather here were chances to interact and communicate during those rare, quiet alert moments that seemed to accompany changing time. There are some products to help you make the most of this precious time.

I used a musical mobile attached to the changing table and it was positioned where Charlie could see it while he was being changed. I had been given a wind-up mobile, which given my state of sleep deprivation, was too energy draining. Next time I would definitely get one with an on-off switch. But be aware, however, most mobiles are usually *wind-up* models in disguise and such a switch merely lets you stop and start the wound-up music box. The trick is to look for one that's *battery-operated*, such as the CribEssentials Mobile (see pages 90-91).

I found the changing table to be a great place to interact with Charlie, to sing and talk to him. Our pediatrician, Dr. Jim Varga, emphasized how important it is to just talk to your baby. That sounds simple enough but I must admit it felt very awkward to do so, particularly since I had little experience around babies. I only wish I had known about **Baby's First Year** (about $14) by Rock-A-Bye Baby.

Baby's First Year is an award-winning, daily learning program for infants that includes interactive games and exercises designed to stimulate a baby's natural learning skills. The format is a large calendar you can hang over the changing table or area that provides fun, easy games for each day to stimulate intellectual, physical and emotional development. It includes large calendar pictures that use colors and graphics designed to interest babies and special "milestone" memory stickers that turn the calendar into a treasured keepsake. Developed by Dr. Norma Jean Stodden, a noted early development specialist, Baby's First Year won the prestigious Parents' Choice Gold Award. Call Rock-

A-Bye Baby (Florida) at **800-ROCK-A-BYE (800/762-5229)** for the nearest retailer or The Baby Club of America (Connecticut) at **(800/752-9736)** for phone orders.

Besides Baby's First Year, I wish I had used the Wimmer-Ferguson high-contrast toys with Charlie, especially during the first few months. Not based on a sudden black-and-white "fad," these are truly pioneering, innovative developmental toys based on educational research as to the visual preferences of babies, including newborns.

Introduced in 1983, the **Infant Stim-Mobile** (about $20 and $26 with additional color cards) was the company's first product. Child development specialist Ruth Wimmer Ferguson designed a mobile (originally for her daughter) that included elements reflecting her review of academic research on infant visual perception. Infant Stim-Mobile comes with five reversible graphic cards, with simple designs on one side and more complex ones on the other. With an emphasis on consumer education, the particularly helpful instruction sheet enclosed with the mobile provides interesting background information on what a new baby sees as

well as many different suggestions on how to use the cards and how to identify your baby's non-verbal communication cues. Other Wimmer-Ferguson toys that I'd also want to have include **Pattern-Play** (about $12.95) cushioned vinyl cards that are great for hanging, standing or easy travel; **Pattern-Pals** (about $19.95) multisensory soft toys; and the large 12-by-16-inch **Double-Feature** scratch resistent safety mirror (about $26.95) (pictured on the next page) that is backed by black and white graphics and installs easily in a crib or playpen. (See also pages 92-93 for more about mirrors.)

Wimmer-Ferguson products have been featured in many major media and have received the following awards: Oppenheim Toy Portfolio honored Infant Stim-Mobile and Double Feature as "Blue Chip Classics" and Pattern-Pals with the 1992 "Platinum Award" (for year's best toys). Wimmer-Ferguson products are available through most toy and baby specialty stores and catalogs (I received a listing of 42 retailers in Los Angeles alone!) and you can certainly call Wimmer-Ferguson (Colorado) at **800/747-2454** for locations near you. (You might also ask them to send you a free copy of the "What Does a Baby See?" article, which is a fascinating, one-page summary of infant visual perception that explains such things as how and when to use high-contrast toys during play time and the importance of including soothing, pastel colors for quiet time.)

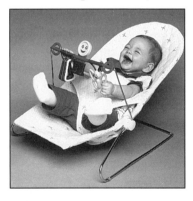

It's also good during wake time (which admittedly can turn quickly into sleep time) to provide different physical surfaces and settings for your newborn baby in the nursery and the rest of the house. I used the **Summer Playtime Soft Seat**™ (about $30 to $35) with Charlie. This is a gentle bouncer seat that includes a two-way restraining system with Velcro® fasteners, a quilted cover that is machine washable and dryable and an educational toybar. I particularly like the toybar on this model because it has bright, bold colors, smiling faces and interesting shapes and sounds that stimulated Charlie. You can also detach both the toybar as well as the individual toys for greater variety and play value. The seat also disassembles for travel or storage. The canopy is an extra accessory on this model (about $10-12). Summer seats are available in U.S. specialty stores, juvenile catalogs and mass merchandisers (K-Mart, Wal-Mart, Target and Toys R Us). You can call Summer Infant Products (Rhode Island) at **800/9BOUNCR (800/926-8627)**.

Swings give babies a change of position, a different view of the world and provide a comforting, soothing motion similar to that felt in the womb. I used a battery-operated swing with Charlie when he was about five weeks old. I wish I had the **Evenflo® Swing** (No. 401166, about $70), which doubles as both

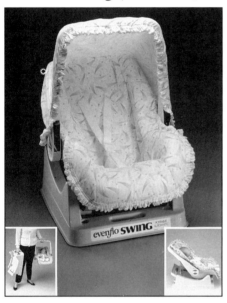

a portable swing and a carrier and can be used for a newborn baby (up through one weighing 16 pounds). The compact design of this swing eliminates cumbersome and space hungry legs. Because it's portable, you can move it around from room to room and put it on the floor. It's easy to get a baby in and out of this swing. Two "D" size batteries will provide up to 150 hours of quiet, gentle, swinging motion. Lifted off the base, the Evenflo Swing also makes a great carrier with its two positions, upright and recline. The handle also has multiple positions and can be used for hanging toys. Made in the U.S., the swing also comes with a canopy that is removable. Call Evenflo (Ohio) at **800/233-5921** to contact a local distributor. (See also floor model swings on page 60.)

I learned about another simple change-of-pace play setting from Mel, a dear lady with four grown children and 10 grandchildren, who helped with Charlie when he was about six weeks old. She suggested laying Charlie on a quilt on the floor, an idea that frankly hadn't occurred to me. Here's a way to make an often unused decorative quilt or comforter into a highly functional item. Charlie still loves the **Red Calliope Comforter** his cousins gave him. Incidentally, Red Calliope was the first company to introduce coordinated bedding to the juvenile products industry. Call Red Calliope (California) at **800/421-0526** for a store near you.

Another wonderful item for floor time is the **Ruggie Bear®** **Activity Play Mat** ($30 to $35) by Century Products Company. It's soft and cuddly like a comforter, but it also has five activity toys—rattle rings, gripper teether, crinkle bow tie, safety mirror and squeaker heart (the first four detach with Velcro® tabs). It

has a machine washable, soft dark blue cotton body and your baby is sure to get a lot of use out of this product designed for babies up to 18 months. The **Century® Busy Bear™ Activity Playmat** ($20 to $22) was just introduced and offers a less expensive, although more brightly colored, high-contrast product. You can't go wrong with either. Call Century (Ohio) at **800/837-4044** for a local store or to order direct.

2

Nursing at Its Best

If you're going to be (or are) breastfeeding, you'll want to read this chapter. Based on my experience as well as the experience of several "lactation" (breastfeeding) consultants and educators I highly respect, I have selected products that help nursing moms meet a variety of different needs. By no means, however, will you need all of the products in this chapter.

If you're going to be a new nursing mother, I urge you to learn as much as possible about breastfeeding *before* your baby's birth and to have the name and number of at least one recommended lactation consultant, who may end up being your best helper. Perhaps the pediatric practice you select has a consultant on staff or can recommend a good one. Ask your childbirth educator for the name of one. Make sure, however, you have someone who's a *certified* lactation consultant (a variety of organizations offer certification programs). You might also contact your local **La Leche League** (Illinois) for breastfeeding information and support (call the national number at **708/455-7730** to get the number for your local chapter or look in the phone book). For me, breastfeeding was a challenging, new experience but a richly rewarding one thanks in large measure to Kittie Frantz, a wonderful lactation expert who was there when Charlie and I needed her.

PILLOWS

Don't put yourself through the agony of positioning pillows you happen to have on hand for breastfeeding and trying to get yourself and your newborn baby into a comfortable and proper alignment. Remember you'll be breastfeeding for several hours each day and you deserve to be as comfortable as possible, as quickly as possible, with the least amount of energy expended on this activity.

I went through about six weeks of agony before I discovered a real lifesaver, the **Nurse Mate** nursing pillow (about $36) from Four Dee Products, (which you use while sitting). Designed by a mother with twins, the Nurse Mate holds your baby(ies) in the ideal nursing position while nestling your baby(ies) in the soft comfort of a five-inch deep convoluted foam cushion. This u-

shaped pillow fits around your waist. Since your baby rests directly on the pillow, instead of on you, muscle strain is relieved on your arms, neck and back. However, if you have a long torso, you should lay a bed pillow on your lap first and then put the Nurse Mate on top of the bed pillow. Otherwise, you may start leaning over to nurse, which isn't a correct nursing position.

Nurse Mate also provides extra protection to C-section incisions. What's more, it can provide hands-free nursing—what a pleasure to be able to read, eat a meal or help another child without having to interrupt your baby's nursing schedule.

Although the pillow comes with a washable, zippered cover, I found it easier to throw a fresh towel or receiving blanket on top of the pillow. Nurse Mate comes with a strap but I didn't need to use it to keep the pillow in place. I was most comfortable using the pillow on a couch with my legs bent and my feet propped up. The La Leche League (Illinois) endorses this pillow and carries it in their international catalog (call **708/451-1891**). You can also call Four Dee Products (Texas) at **800/526-2594** for a local distributor or to order direct.

I just learned of another handy pillow that could have helped when I was breastfeeding in bed. It's called the **Pregnancy Wedge**, Model P-100 ($13 to $15) by Body Therapeutics and is a multi-purpose support device that can be used in your bed during pregnancy and after (when you're lying on your side). It's

also useful after a C-section (or any abdominal surgery) to support a swollen abdomen. Call Body Therapeutics (California) at **310/945-8141** for a distributor or to order direct. Body Therapeutics also carries back support pillows.

PUMPS

You will probably want to have at least one breast pump, if for no other reason than to have an emergency supply of milk on hand in the freezer. There are other reasons as well, such as building or maintaining your milk supply if you're a working mother who will be away from your baby for many hours a day and also, to relieve engorged breasts if your baby isn't able to nurse sufficiently. If possible, use a pump that offers "double pumping," i.e., pumping both breasts at the same time, because your pumping time will be cut in half—especially important if you're a working mother,.

As one lactation expert puts it, pumping is a "con job" that mimics what a baby does. The pumps included here are the best mimics in the marketplace. Let's start with the most inexpensive and move up from there.

There are two excellent *hand pumps* from which to choose that are safe, apply no painful pressure and use a "one-pump-per-second" rhythm or cycle, the ideal rhythm that mimics what a baby does. These hand pumps are inexpensive, handy, lightweight and easy to use. I used the **Manual Breastpump** by Medela, Type S, #50012 (about $25). It comes with a durable bottle but you can use any standard bottle or a freezer bag (inside a bottle) with this pump. (Try not to transfer pumped milk into another container because every time you do so, bacteria can increase.) Call Medela (Illinois) at **800/435-8316** to order direct or contact the La Leche League International Catalog (Illinois) at **708/451-1891** to order.

 Next time I would look at the **One-Hand Breast Pump** (about $25) by Ameda/Egnell which offers one-hand convenience and the ability to pump directly into a freezer bag as well as a bottle. I like the easy-to-read printed measurements on the four-ounce bottle that's included. Call Ameda/Egnell (Illinois) **800/323-8750** for a local distributor or to order direct. See also the "Cool 'n Carry Pump 'n Save System" on page 71 in Chapter 7.

There is no "best" in the battery pump category. They are all pretty much the same. A battery pump may be ideal if you're a working mother without a private office or work space. Even without an outlet, you can use it in the bathroom. However, you shouldn't use a battery pump, which is a less natural, "draw and hold" pump, if you're trying to build your milk supply; rather it's for a woman who has extra milk and has no trouble "letting down" (the reflexive surging or ejection of milk at the start of nursing or pumping).

Besides hand and battery pumps, there are also more powerful electric pumps. The **Nurture III Small Electric Breast Pump** by Ameda/Egnell (No. 3512, about $105) is a portable pump that is economical yet efficient. It weighs less than a pound, is quiet and can provide double pumping (which cuts pumping time). This is a "draw and hold" pump. Call Ameda/Egnell (Illinois) at **800/323-8750** for a local distributor or to order direct.

The next three electric pumps are larger rental units and each offers double pumping, the ideal one-pump-per-second rhythm and a relaxing, quiet sound. They're helpful for building your milk supply. Ameda/Egnell has a medium electric pump, the **Lact-E Lightweight Electric Piston Breast Pump**, which weighs 11 pounds (the lightest weight of all the rental pumps that have the one-pump-per-second rhythm). Their top-of-the-line pump is the heavy, hospital-quality **SMB Electric Piston Breast Pump**.

I rented Medela's **Classic™ Breastpump** shown on page 22 and purchased the **Universal Pumping System** accessory kit (No. 61027, about $38.70) to go with it (which includes the Medela® Manual Breastpump). I was happy using this heavy duty,

efficient, easy-to-use, quiet model at home, although I didn't pump as often as I had planned. For **breast pump rental stations**, try any of the following: ask your childbirth educator; call Medela (Illinois) at **800/TELLYOU (800/835-5968)** for their 24-hour "Breastfeeding National Network" service, which will give you three breast pump rental stations nearest your zip code (plus a few lactation professional referrals); call Ameda/Egnell (Illinois) at **800/323-8750**; or call the La Leche League (Illinois) at **708/455-7730** for your local La Leche League chapter that should have names of rental stations. See also Chapter 7, pages 70-71, for special tote bags to carry breastfeeding equipment and gear.

SPECIAL HELPERS

My husband and I had a wonderful Lamaze instructor, Louise Tellalian, who provided an extensive "lending library" of educational materials during her eight-week program. Among the videos we checked out were several in the outstanding series **"Breastfeeding Techniques That Work!™"** which were written and produced by Kittie Frantz, R.N., C.P.N.P. and are available from Geddes Productions. This series presents a very positive approach to breastfeeding in a modular learning program with different subjects on each video.

I have personally seen and highly recommend: "First Attachment" (Volume 1), "First Attachment in Bed" (Volume 2) and "Burping the Baby" (Volume 4). Other important titles in the series include "First Attachment After Cesarean" (Volume 3), "Successful Working Mothers" (Volume 5), "Hand Expression" (Volume 6) and "Supplemental Nursing System" (Volume 7). The average viewing time per video is a comfortable 15 to 20 minutes. Generally, hospitals and educators buy these tapes and make them available to patients and students. Ask your childbirth and pediatric professionals about them. You can also buy them direct at about $40 each from Geddes Productions (California), **818/951-2809**.

Seeing such videos, especially repeatedly, and practicing the correct positioning and attachment as shown in the videos should in most cases prevent sore nipples. If you haven't been exposed to these videos or some other good breastfeeding education and you end up with sore nipples, you may find **Lansinoh®** **for**  **Nursing Mothers** (about $10), the purest, pesticide-free, hypoallergenic lanolin, to be soothing and healing. It's available from the La Leche League International Catalog (Illinois) at **708/451-1891** and One Step Ahead (Illinois) at **800/274-8440** or by calling Lansinoh Laboratories (Tennessee) at **800/292-4794** for the name of a local drug store or health food store. (Never use Vitamin E oil because it's toxic to babies.) And of course, you'll want to contact a lactation consultant immediately. Don't give up!

The La Leche League is an excellent source for breastfeeding information, referrals to local support groups, nursing products and educational materials. La Leche has many books on breast-feeding and they publish *The Womanly Art of Breastfeeding* (about $10), which is considered by many to be the best book on breastfeeding. (It's also available in bookstores.)

You may need nursing pads for your bra if you leak breast milk. (I bought them before I went to the hospital but ended up not needing them.) Pads come in disposable as well as reusable (washable) styles. Both disposables and reusables may or may not come with a moisture-proof barrier that is made of such materials as plastic, nylon or rayon, which make it more difficult for milk to penetrate the pad. You might want to avoid this kind of pad if you have sore nipples or your baby has thrush because accu-mulated moisture may make these conditions worse.

Johnson's Nursing Pads (about $3 for 36 pads) are small, thick, disposable pads with a self-stick adhesive that keeps them in place. Made of polyester and rayon, this pad is ideal for a working woman because it won't leak easily.

It's better to start in the beginning with a non-barrier type that breathes such as Ameda/Egnell's **Nursing Pads**, No. R3595 (about $9 for three pairs). They are thick and soft, 100 percent cotton, very absorbent and washable. For availability see Ameda/Egnell on page 22.

If you leak heavily, go through pads quickly or are a working woman in a visible or public position where you can't risk get-ting your blouse wet, look at *breast shells*, sometimes called *breast cups*. (Do not confuse these with *nipple shields*, which are very dangerous to use.) Ameda/Egnell's **Breast Shell System** (about $14) is the best for catching leaks for a working woman and the cotton roll insert can hold up to two ounces of milk.

Breast shells are also useful for protecting sore nipples by preventing them from rubbing against your bra. Ameda/Egnell's breast shell has an adapter for just this purpose.

I hope you never need to use one of my favorite products, the *feeding tube device.* Medela's device, called the **Supplemental Nursing System**™ or simply SNS™ (No. 00901S, about $37), was a lifesaver that enabled me to continue breastfeeding Charlie

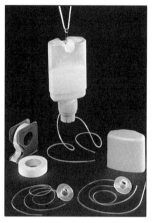 who turned out to be an "ineffective nurser." The SNS functioned as a kind of training wheels that helped him to suck and swallow correctly. A versatile product, SNS can keep babies on the breast when they need supplemental feedings and can be used with premature babies; weak, ineffective or lazy nursers; adopted babies; babies with weak suckling; and low milk supply mothers. I also found SNS useful later on, when long after I had stopped using it, I became engorged and used it to relieve the engorgement, which Charlie wasn't able to do through normal nursing. (See page 22 for information on Kittie Frantz's video on SNS.) Call Medela (Illinois) at **800/435-8316** to order the SNS direct.

3

The Best Bottles
and Accessories

You'll want to read this chapter if you're planning to use bottles
with your baby right from the start or at some point in the
future.

If you're planning to breastfeed, your baby may never touch
a bottle. Some babies go straight to a cup when they are weaned.
Some babies will both nurse and take a bottle. And some will
only be bottle fed.

NIPPLES

If you nurse, it's recommended that you shouldn't introduce a
bottle, at least for a month, maybe longer, otherwise "nipple con-
fusion" can set in and the baby may just opt out for the bottle,
which for some babies is easier than the breast.

I waited a couple of months before even trying to introduce
a bottle because there was a good chance Charlie was one of
those babies who would have willingly given up the breast for
the bottle.

Much to my amazement, however, when I introduced a bottle
he rejected it. I tried different latex nipples and a nurser bottle
but he flatly refused. Then one day, while reading my *What to
Expect the First Year* bible, I came across the idea of trying a
silicone nipple. Sure enough, it worked and Charlie gladly took

his first bottle with a Pur Silicone Nipple at about three months. I really like the Playskool® **Pur® Silicone Nipples** (about $2.70) because they are durable, odorless and come in different sizes and for different ages. I also like the Playskool bottles because the size markings are printed in dark blue and are easy to read. Playskool bottles and nipples are available at mass merchandise stores or call Playskool (Rhode Island) at **401/431-TOYS (401/431-8697)**.

You may want to use a *nurser bottle*, sometimes also called a *disposable bottle* because you dispose of the plastic bottle liners (and don't have to wash bottles) and you can squeeze more air out of the bottle liner (and supposedly the baby swallows less gas-causing air). But if your baby doesn't like the nipple on this type of bottle (as Charlie didn't), try **The First Years® Nipple Adapter**, No. 1010 (about $2). It lets you use standard size nipples on nursers. For store locations, call The First Years/Kiddie Products, Inc. (Massachusetts) at **800/533-6708**.

BOTTLE ACCESSORIES

If you do choose a nurser bottle, here's one patented accessory that can make it easy to remove air from the disposable bottle

liner. Use **The Bottle Burper®** ($1.40 to $2) instead of tediously squeezing the air out with your fingers. It's available by mail order through The Right Start Catalog (California) at **800-548-8531** and One Step Ahead (Illinois) at **800/274-8440** or call Tender Moments (Georgia) at **404/365-9090** for local store names.

Before your baby learns to hold a bottle, try the **Freehand® Bottle Holder** (about $4) by Leachco, which features a patented,

comfortable handle that lets you feed a bottle to your baby with one hand, leaving you a free hand for tending to another child or tending to yourself. Durable and dishwasher safe, it simply snaps directly onto any conventionally shaped bottle. Call Leachco (Oklahoma) at **800/525-1050** for catalogs or local stores or to order direct.

BOTTLES

Learning to hold a bottle by himself was undoubtedly one of Charlie's greatest early accomplishments symbolizing both his independence, ability to comfort himself and the development of his "gross motor" coordination (see also page 103). I was able to teach him in less than a week how to do this at about 5½ months. Charlie was able to learn with an ordinary four-ounce bottle.

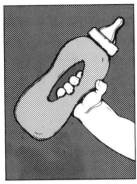 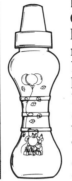 But I bet I could have cut Charlie's training time in half if I had discovered what have become my favorite bottles, the änsa® Easy-To-Hold® Bottle (with the hole in the middle) and the änsa® Baby Care® Infant Grip® Bottle ($2.50 to $3). They're designed to be held by a baby's little hand. They both come in four-ounce and eight-ounce sizes in a variety of wonderful colors and graphics. Beautiful as well as functional, the patented änsa Easy-To-Hold Bottle is included in the Design Collection of The Museum of Modern Art. änsa bottles, which are made in the U.S., are available through most major chains such as Wal-Mart, K-Mart, Target and Toys R Us. For local store locations, you can call änsa Company Customer Service (Oklahoma) at 918/687-1664. (By the way, änsa makes its own baby bottle brush for about $1.29 that is specially designed for their bottles but can be used to clean nearly every baby bottle. I've used this brush and it works great.)

Also consider the Kinder-Grip™ bottle by Playtex® (about $3), which is a new, patented bottle that has a leakproof cap, flat sides to resist rolling and a compact shape for easy travel. It's available at any Toys R Us and other large food, drug or mass merchandise stores or call Playtex at 800/222-0453 (or in New Jersey, 800/624-0825.)

Bottle Hoods and Caps
If you end up with a lot of different bottles, some of which have no *hoods* (caps), you may want to buy hood and *collar* (the part that holds the nipple) sets. (Hoods help keep the nipple cleaner and maintain freshness.) I like the Gerber® Collars and Snap Off Hoods (No. 76107, about 80 cents for two sets) which are durable and made in the U.S. The hood snaps off with one hand for convenience at feeding time and accommodates different size nipples on standard bottles. Call Gerber (Michigan) at 800/4-

GERBER (800/443-7237) for stores that are likely to carry their hoods and collars as well as their bottles, which are also durable.

WASHING AND STORAGE ACCESSORIES

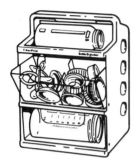

With bottle feeding come many parts to wash and store. I use several organizers that manage these parts. The **Fisher-Price® Bottle Organizer** (No. 1520, about $15) holds and dispenses up to six bottles; stores nipples, pacifiers, hoods and collars; and has a built-in bottle liner dispenser (if you use nurser bottles). Major retailers such as Toys R Us, Wal-Mart, K-Mart and Target carry this organizer or call Fisher-Price (New York) at **800/432-KIDS (800/432-5437)**.

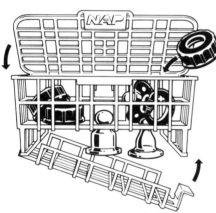

Prince Lionheart makes two bottle sanitizing/storage devices I use right in my dishwasher. The handy **NAP® Nipple and Pacifier Sanitizing Device** (about $8.50) features two plastic baskets in one that securely hold nipples, pacifiers, collars, hoods and other small feeding items for dishwasher cleaning. The patented, unique twin-lid design features a fully contained upper basket for small items while up to eight nipples are help upright by the lower lid enclosure right above the water source for thorough sanitizing and cleaning.

SANI-STOR™ (about $9) is a complete sanitizing and storage system for baby bottles that you can use in your dishwasher, on your counter (to air dry and/or store bottles) or on a shelf (mounted as a space-saving, sliding bottle dispenser). Call Prince Lionheart at **800/544-1132** (805/922-2250 in California) for a local store or to mail order these products, which are made in the U.S. (On the top of the next page is a photo showing a dishwasher containing both the Nipple and Pacifier Sanitizing Device (NAP) and the SANI-STOR.)

The **Bottle Dryer** (about $12) by Pearcy Company is a very

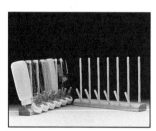handy device we use for air drying and storing six bottles and their nipples and collars. It's made of solid rock maple and finished with non-toxic, FDA-approved materials. It's a high-precision product that uses "wooden boat technology." Pearcy Company makes all their own dowels and doesn't use any glue. Call this Ohio-based company at **419/636-4193** for dealer names.

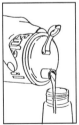If you're using bottles, you may be using formula. I wish I had had these three products. One is **Pour & Store Formula Caps** (No. 280, about $2 for two) by Safety 1st. I haven't tested this new product but it features a "snap-close" spout that should make pouring easy. It fits both 13-ounce and 32-ounce formula cans. For store locations, call Safety 1st (Massachusetts) at **800/962-7233**.

I preferred using prepared formula but had I known about the next two items, I might have considered dry formula more seriously. I have examined the three-compartment **Powdered**

Milk Container (about $10) and found the top turns easily to each compartment but is a little difficult to remove (which may be a safety feature). It's available from The Maya Group (California) at **714/898-0807**.

Be on the lookout for a three-compartment container by Marshall Baby Products that doubles either as a powdered formula container or a snack container. Called the **MagMag® Insti-Snack™ Powdered Formula/Snack Container** (No. D792, about $8), it has three individual compartments that stack on top of each other. It measures 5 3/8 inches high by 2¾ inches in diameter. Call Marshall Baby Products (Illinois) at **800/634-4350** for a store in your area.

For middle-of-the-night bottle feedings I wish I had known about Playskool Baby's **Easy Feedin'™ Nighttime Feeder™** (No. 3511, about $45). A removable thermal cooler keeps two pre-chilled bottles cool until a baby wakes. Then the steamer warms bottles to the proper temperature in minutes. Keep the feeder in the nursery or in your bedroom. For availability of this product call Playskool (Rhode Island) at **401/431-TOYS (401/431-8697)**.

4

The Best
Mealtime Mates

Mealtime for baby brings many surprises, not the least of which is the number of things you'll probably want such as a high chair, feeding items, organizers and some healthful, prepared foods, not to mention the on-the-go mealtime products that are covered in Chapter 7 on pages 75-77.

HIGH CHAIRS
Mealtime with food starts to get serious at around six months. That's the time you'll want to have a high chair.

I happen to really like high chairs with wheels because we have wood floors and I like to move Charlie around—to the table to be near us when we're eating, closer to the television to watch "Sesame Street" during breakfast or to the kitchen for cleanups. When I went to the JPMA trade show I found very few high chairs with wheels, in part because manufacturers are afraid of liability and also because consumers aren't demanding them. If your baby has an older (but immature) sibling who would like to take your baby out for a test drive in the high chair, you may prefer the stationary models. But two of the three models I'm recommending also come equipped with brakes.

I've been very happy with my **Peg Perego High Chair/Youth Chair** (No. 21-01-027, about $119). I like the six adjustable heights

and the roomy tray that's adjustable to three positions. There's a high backrest, a wide base for stability, a handle at the back that works great as a bib/towel holder and a removable seat that can be used as a play seat. The **Deluxe High Chair** (No. 21-01-028, about $139) pictured here has more padded comfort plus brakes on the back wheels (although there are also plans to add rear brakes to the regular chair just described). The tray is not quite as large. I like the Peg Perego quality built into both these Italian high chairs, both of which are also JPMA certified. For a distributor, call Peg Perego U.S.A. (Indiana) at **219/484-3093**.

I also recommend the **Home & Roam™ Double Duty High Chair** (about $135) by Baby Trend®, which I've been testing. It

has a six-position height adjustment and a one-hand removable tray that hangs on the side of the chair when not in use. There are brakes on all four wheels. I like the way I can adjust the tray up close to Charlie so that fewer pieces of food drop down. The tray is a little high for him, though, because it has a high lip (which probably also acts as a food barrier). The removable seat doubles as a handy hook-on chair, which you can use with or without the tray. There is a handy bar for a bib or towel.

The Home & Roam is available by mail order through The Right Start Catalog (California) at **800/548-8531**, One Step Ahead (Illinois) at **800/274-8440** and the J.C. Penney catalog and their retail stores. You can also call Baby Trend (California) at **800/421-1902**.

If you don't need or want a high chair with wheels, consider the **Fisher-Price® Deluxe High Chair** (No. 9126, about $50). This high chair features a one-hand, push button large tray with many adjustments, three-position footrest, towel and bib bar and a double-lock release for easy folding and compact storage. Many of my friends use this high chair and really love it. Major retailers such as Toys R Us, Wal-Mart, K-Mart and Target carry Fisher-Price brand products or call Fisher-Price (New York) at **800/432-KIDS** (**800/432-5437**) for a store near you.

BIBS

When you first start feeding your baby solid food, you're going to need a feeding bib. My favorite bib is the **Bumkins Waterproof Bib** (about $4 for regular size, which Charlie wears,

$7 for junior). You don't need a lot of these bibs because they're made of a unique, lightweight, waterproof-treated fabric that wipes or rinses off easily and air dries quickly. (They're also machine washable and dryable on low.) Unlike plastic or vinyl, this fabric won't crack or peel, is comfortable to wear and resists most stains and odors. Velcro® closures (the only way to go in bibs) provide a quick and adjustable fit and a crumb catcher pocket (also a must) collects spills that would otherwise go onto a baby's lap or the seat of the chair. The patterns are colorful and fun and don't fade even after extensive washing. The bib is available through retail stores nationally (call Bumkins in Arizona at **602/254-2626**) or order through mail order from The Right Start Catalog (California) at **800/526-5220**, and ask for "Super Bibs."

MEALTIME FEEDING AND STORAGE ITEMS

I like many Playskool Baby mealtime feeding items, especially the **Scooper® Plate** (No. 3068, about $3.20) and **Scooper® Bowl** (No. 3067, about $3.20) because they have a special curved rim that guides food onto the spoon and they have suction ring bases for attaching them to a high chair tray. The **Easy Grip®** **Fork and Spoon** (No. 3035, about $1.50) have special looped handles that are easier for a young baby to grasp (you can buy the spoon separately, too). I haven't tested the **Soft Scoop Spoon™** (No. 3021, $1.50) which is brand new but its flexible, rounded tip looks ideal for a baby's tender gums and for scooping out food in those hard-to-reach areas in baby jars and containers.

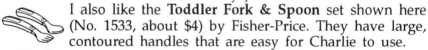 I also like the **Toddler Fork & Spoon** set shown here (No. 1533, about $4) by Fisher-Price. They have large, contoured handles that are easy for Charlie to use.

Finding microwavable baby bowls and dishes can be challenging, in part because manufacturers are afraid that consumers will heat food incorrectly and/or not properly test for hot spots that can occur and cause serious burns. With that in mind, here are a few that are microwavable. Playskool's **Microwave Warm 'n Serve™ Dish** (No. 3470, about $4), features a carry handle, three compartments, a clear, tilt-up cover and the Scooper® rim. **The First Years® Sure-Grip Suction Bowl With Lid** (No. 1625A, about $3.30) is a handy small bowl (but be sure not to microwave the lid or suction ring). For product availability call Playskool (Rhode Island) at **401/431-TOYS (401/431-8697)** and call The First Years (Massachusetts) at **800/533-6708**.

 You can always use durable **Rubbermaid Servin' Saver™** containers for microwaving food that you transfer to your baby's bowl or plate. The ten-ounce (about $1.30) and four-ounce (about $2 for two) Servin' Saver Cylinders are my favorites. (The four-ounce containers are shown here.) They're handy, can be used in the freezer and because they're completely leak-proof, are great for travel.

If the microwavable feature isn't that important and you prefer instead darling graphics that can be educational and fun for developing verbal communication as well as healthy mealtime attitudes, look at some of the exciting melamine dinnerware sets that are available. I particularly like those offered in the **Lillian Vernon® Catalog**. The barnyard pattern you see here may not be available forever but you can count on equally wonderful designs. Fully coordinated, the four-piece dinnerware set (about $15) offers matching flatware fork and spoon (about $5) and a 40-inch-square vinyl mat (about $10). Contact Lillian Vernon (Virginia) at **804/430-5555** to order direct.

CUPS

When your baby is ready to start using a cup, I recommend the **Advanced MagMag™ Training Cup System** (No. D775, about $20) from Marshall Baby Products. This is a four-step learning system Charlie uses that includes interchangeable accessories to teach a baby or toddler how to drink independently from a cup. There are four types of cups you can create: a nursing cup (with a silicone nipple), a spout cup, a straw cup and a training cup with a removable slow-flow insert. There's a simple chart on the box showing suggested age ranges for the cups. Each of the durable and adorable cups can be used with or without the removable handles. No-leak covers and lid are also included. The straw is unfortunately too long for Charlie to use when he's in his high chair. Accessories can also be purchased separately. Go to Toys R Us or call Marshall (Illinois) at **800/634-4350** for juvenile specialty retailers in your area (which could probably order this product for you.)

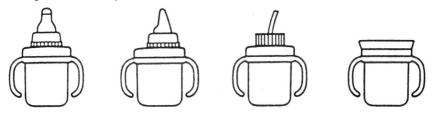

Charlie has used two other training cups I like because the flow is slower than most training cups in which the liquid comes out too fast, spilling over everything and frustrating both baby and parent. The **Flow Control Cup** (No. 1526, about $4) by Fisher-Price lets me adjust the flow from "low" to "high" as Charlie has learned to drink better. Major retailers such as Toys R Us, Wal-Mart, K-Mart and Target carry the Fisher-Price brand or call Fisher-Price (New York) **800/432-KIDS (800/432-5437)** for a store near you.

The **Cherubs Collection Training Cup** (about $3.20) by Playtex® has only one small hole, which is perfect for a slow flow. This cup also comes in 12 darling designs (Charlie has enjoyed the Dalmatians and fire engine design). This U.S.-made cup is available at any Toys R Us, food/drug/mass retail chains and infant specialty stores.

I haven't tested Playskool's new **Drip-less Cups** (No. 3054, about $3.80) but they look like a good idea considering how much fun Charlie has had turning cups over to watch the liquid drip out. (On the other hand, you'd give up a good science lesson on gravity.)

FOOD STORAGE AND PREPARATION ACCESSORIES

If you're using jars of baby food, you'll want to get Prince Lionheart's **UFO, Universal Food Organizer** (No. 2001, about

$14), which is a U.S.-made, versatile storage carousel we use that adjusts up and down for maximum space utilization. This quality carousel rotates freely and can later be used to hold small cans and jars for the whole family. An additional storage tier called **UFO Stages** (No. 2003, $7 to $8) is now available, too. Call Prince Lionheart at **800/544-1132** (805/922-2250 in California) for a local store or to order direct.

If you prefer grinding your own table food for your baby, Marshall's patented **Happy Baby® Deluxe Food Grinder With Tote** (No. 800A, about $12) is easy to use, economical and

healthier, provided you use fresh natural foods. You simply place food in the cylinder and gently pull the cylinder down to force food through a precision-sharpened, stainless steel blade and strainer into a four-ounce feeding dish. It was developed by a pediatrician and is dishwasher safe. It's available at Toys R Us or call Marshall (Illinois) at **800/634-4350** for juvenile specialty retailers in your area.

FAVORITE PREPARED FOODS

I found a number of commercially prepared food products to be convenient to use and of very high quality.

Since I needed to supplement my breastfeeding, I selected a quality formula that was readily available in markets and drug stores—**Enfamil®**. For convenience, I only bought the ready-to-use cans. I had a couple of opportunities to call the manufacturer, Mead Johnson Nutritionals, and found the company to be helpful and cooperative. In researching this book, I received Mead Johnson information emphasizing that breastfeeding is the best method for feeding babies and that mothers should consult with their physician before deciding to use formula. I appreciate their concerned and honest approach to consumer education—this is a company I can trust.

My favorite baby food is **Earth's Best** because it tastes good and only uses certified organically grown ingredients without any  synthetic pesticides. To ensure that natural flavors and nutrients aren't compromised in processing, Earth's Best only uses whole foods for ingredients and never adds any salt, sugar or starches. Of the complete line of 41 foods, Charlie has particularly enjoyed the fruit and vegetable purees, juices and whole grain cereals. Earth's Best baby foods cost a little more (about 60 to 70 cents a jar) but I feel they are well worth it (I get a substantial discount from one store when I buy a case at a time). They're available in supermarkets in a third of the U.S., in natural food stores and by mail order by calling Earth's Best (Vermont) at **800/442-4221**.

 Though not organic, **Gerber®** **3ᴿᴰ FOODS™ Fruit and Veggie Juices** (about 61 to 65 cents) are a wonderful alternative to plain fruit juices and have no added sugar. The suggested age on the label reads "from about 9 months." Per our pediatrician's recommendation, we try to limit all juices to meal-time (at the end of a meal). Charlie likes the "Apple Carrot" and the "Apple Sweet Potato." I'm sure he'd also like the "Orange Carrot" as well as the "Pineapple Carrot" but I haven't seen these in the market yet. If your market doesn't yet carry these juices, ask them to order them for you.

 When I started to give Charlie solid food, I selected early foods with a high "meltability" factor. Like most parents, I gave him Cheerios® brand Os but I soon switched to U.S. Mills **Erewhon® Super O's Oat Bran Rings** (about $3), which are sweetened with fruit juice and are wheat-free and salt-free. I also like their **Erewhon Banana O's** and **Apple Stroodles™** (which are each $3.35 and $3.49). U.S. Mills products are at natural food stores nationwide and selected supermarkets.

One of Charlie's first words was "coo-coo" short for "cookie."

The first cookies and crackers I willingly gave him were those made by **Health Valley®**. They are made with whole grain flours, some of which are organic, are sweetened with sulfite-free fruit juice and honey and aren't made with white flour, hydrogenated shortening, preservatives, sugar and salt. Our favorites (I eat them, too!) are the **Oat Bran Graham Crackers**, the **Amaranth Graham Crackers, Stoned Wheat Crackers, Healthy Grahams™ Animal Cookies** and **Fat-Free Raspberry Fruit Centers™ Cookies**. The graham crackers are about $2.10 a box and the cookies are about $2.45. We also like their organic soups. Nine types are avail-

able and our favorites are **Minestrone** and **Vegetable**. Health Valley products are available at most major grocery chains in the U.S. and at health food stores. You can call Health Valley (California) at **800/423-4846** to talk to a trained and courteous customer service rep who'll happily give you local store names (Health Valley was cited in *The Wall Street Journal* for its exceptional customer service). The company also has a cash rebate program that rewards loyal customers (and they won't rent out your name either).

Charlie also enjoys **Healthy Times® Arrowroot Cookies for Toddlers** (about $1.80) that are made with arrowroot flour for tender tummies and sweetened with low-acid fruit juice. I really like the Maple Arrowroot Cookies that are wheat-free and "meltable." We've recently discovered Healthy Times **Hugga Bears** cookies (about $2.24), which are made with real fruit pieces and organic grains and include three different adorable bear shapes. Healthy Times (California) also makes two organic instant baby cereals, **Oatmeal with Banana** and **Brown Rice** (about $2.59). Healthy

Times products are available at most health food stores in the U.S. and Canada and some grocery stores. You can call Healthy Times directly at **619/464-1622** if you have any difficulty obtaining a product.

MISCELLANY

Finally, if you're inclined to cook your own fresh, healthful foods but don't know where to begin, aren't sure what's age appropriate and would like specific guidelines, recipes and menu planning, get a copy of *Baby Let's Eat!* (about $9) by Rena Coyle, published by Workman Publishing. My friend Kim gave me this helpful book, which shows you how to adapt meals to your baby and the rest of the family at one sitting. There are four chapters devoted specifically to different ages: 6 to 12 months; 12 to 18 months; 18 to 24 months; and 24 to 36 months.

5

The Best Bath

The bathroom is certainly a place you'll be spending a lot of time with your baby and especially your toddler. In this chapter you will find bath and bathroom equipment and accessories, towels, personal and dental care products and bath toys.

EQUIPMENT AND ACCESSORIES

I remember standing in Toys R Us, looking at infant bath tubs and trying to decide which one to get. I selected the **Fisher-****Price® Bath Center** (No. 9119, about $17), because I wanted the convenience of a tub that would fit in my kitchen sink (it fits either a one- or two-cavity sink). I liked the two, built-in storage compartments that can hold the included soap dish and rinse pitcher with pouring spout as well as water and washcloths. Check availability of this tub at major retailers such as Toys R Us, Wal-Mart, K-Mart and Target or call Fisher-Price (New York) at **800/432-KIDS** for stores near you.

I didn't want a big baby tub because I had no place to put it other than our bathtub (and with enclosed shower doors I didn't want to do gymnastics in order to bathe Charlie). If you

40

don't mind leaning over to wash your baby or you have enough counter space, consider a larger tub such as the **Fisher-Price Soft**  **Spray Tub** (No. 9128, about $20), which comes, as shown here, with a hand-held bath sprayer that makes rinsing your baby easy and a built-in headrest. The sprayer snaps onto the side of the tub for easy storage. Also look at the **Gerry® Two Years® Bath** (No. 465, about $18), which has a special insert for infants. See Fisher-Price in the last paragraph. Call Gerry (Colorado) at **800/525-2472** for a store in your area.

In my research for the book, I came across a versatile product you can use in a bathtub that doesn't have shower doors and that isn't being used by adults. The product is called the **Bathe & Change** (about $438) by Baby Bjorn and is a combination baby  bathtub and changing table (similar to a "bathinett," which my mother used with me in the 50s). Both the bathtub and the changing table are at a convenient work height. Having direct access to running water is especially handy at the changing table. You install the Bathe & Change onto the edges of a bathtub that ideally has a hose with a shower head for added convenience. When you install this 30-pound unit, plan to leave it in position. The width adjusts up to 30 inches, the height adjusts from 14 to 23 inches, the bath tub is 25 by 15 inches and the changing surface, which is enclosed with three high side walls, is 28½ by 28½ inches. The changing table portion is made of a special heat reflective vinyl that warms to the touch in six seconds. A freestanding version costs about $398. Call Baby Bjorn (Georgia) at **800/593-5522** for a local store.

 When Charlie outgrew the infant tub and before he had good head control, I decided to take baths with him in our regular bathtub, following the instructions Jeanne Miller gives in her wonderful book, *The Perfectly Safe® Home* on page 73 (see Chapter 6, page 51, for more information about this book). I use a great bathtub cushion that fits over the side of our tub. It's called the **Polliwog™ Bathtub Sidewall Cushion** and it makes getting in and out of a tub safer. It's also comfortable to sit on and is easy to put on and

take off. It comes in two sizes, 38 inches long (about $30) for a standard bathtub and 16 inches long (about $25) for one with shower doors (the one we have). U.S.-made, the Polliwog received the Seal of Approval from The National Parenting Center (see page 142) in 1992. You can order this product directly from Safe Care Products (Michigan) at **800/733-3004** or through the Perfectly Safe Catalog (Ohio) at **800/837-KIDS (800/837-5437)** or the Safety Solutions Catalog (Texas) at **512/327-2824**.

Once Charlie had good head control, we put him in the **Safety 1st Swivel Bath Seat** (No. 160, about $15) shown here. The swiveling feature makes Charlie accessible, even for those difficult-to-reach areas. The four suction cups keep the seat securely attached. I also found the **Safety 1st Bath Pal** (No. 162, about $3) was useful, especially in the beginning, to test bath water temperature. Contact Safety 1st (Massachusetts) at **800/962-7233** for local store locations.

I'm excited about an innovative piece of bathroom equipment that's not a bath item, although it's used over the bathtub edge. Called **Sinkadink, the Kid's Sink** (about $15) by The Newborne

Company, it's for toddlers. Charlie prefers this innovative, more stable alternative to standing precariously on a step stool trying to reach the big sink. U.S.-made Sinkadink attaches firmly to any bathtub edge and fits over shower door tracks. This adorable miniature sink has places for soap, towel, cup and toothbrush and has an optional mirror (about $5) you'll want to get, too. Order this product through the Perfectly Safe Catalog (Ohio) at **800/837-KIDS (800/837-5437)**.

For sure footing, Charlie uses the Prince Lionheart **SLIP-NOT MAT** (No. 0590, $5 to $6) on our bathroom tile floor next to the Sinkadink. This versatile, high-friction pad (18 by 18 inches) provides a safe, anti-slip surface that also fits securely under a step stool, a potty chair or baby tub that you put on a counter. Call Prince Lionheart at **800/544-1132** (805/922-2250 in California) for a local store or to mail order this product, which is made in the U.S.

As for potties, we're in the early stages of training but have thus far been pleased with the **Century 4-Way Potty Trainer** (No. 9660, $25 to $30). This product can be used as a stand alone potty, a toddler play seat, a step stool and a step-up transitional potty trainer. So far, it's testing successfully in the first two uses. (We haven't yet tested the last two uses yet.) I like the versatility of the product as well as the wide stable base, which is an essential feature. (For more information about potty selection and training, see Katie Van Pelt's helpful book, *Potty Training Your Baby*, which is described in Chapter 12 on page 137. For portable potties, see Chapter 7, pages 77-78.)

I'm looking forward to testing **My Potty Game** (about $18) by Rock-A-Bye Baby, which was designed for ages two and up by an early childhood educator and mother. This looks like a fun, motivational and pressure-free game that rewards positive behavior, builds self-esteem and teaches colors and matching skills at the same time. Subtitled "Toilet Training Made Easy™," this activity game is made in the U.S. Call Rock-A-Bye Baby (Florida) at **800-ROCK-A-BYE (800/762-5229)** for the nearest retailer or call The Baby Club of America (Connecticut) at **800/PLAYPEN (800/752-9736)** to order by phone.

TOWELS

I have four favorite U.S.-made towels that we use (and of course, all are washer/dryer safe). Two are by Rock-A-Bye Baby and are ideal for a tiny infant as well as an older baby. The **Classic EasyDry® Baby Towel** (No. CL600, about $29), is a patented bath towel apron that you wear to keep your clothes dry while bathing your baby and to safely pick up, cuddle and dry your dripping wet baby without fear of the towel slipping. Made of a plush, 12-ounce cotton terry velour, this towel also comes in a less-plush, 9-ounce terry that is a little less expensive (about $25) and is called the **Basic Easy Dry** (No. BA600).

You should have at least one hooded towel and Rock-A-Bye Baby's **Classic FancyDry® Hooded Towel** (No. CL610, about $27) is as beautiful with its satin trim and plush 12-ounce terry as it is practical and absorbent. It's great when we wash Charlie's hair. It also comes with a matching washcloth. All items in the Rock-a-Bye Baby Bathtime Baby

Collection are beautifully sewn and crafted. *Be on the lookout for* their **Bath, Bed'n'Beach Reversible, Hooded Robe** ($30 to $35), which is a new addition that I've seen in their catalog. Call Rock-A-Bye Baby (Florida) at **800-ROCK-A-BYE, 800/762-5229** for the nearest retailer.

To make bath time a fun time we also enjoy the **Li'l Hoodl'ems™** Hooded Towel ($7 to $8) by Gerber. The hood comes in a choice of six darling animal faces and features: cat, rabbit, duck, dog, bear and pig. All except the duck have ears (but the duck has a bill). Made of soft knit cotton terrycloth, the towel measures 30 by 36 inches. It's available at mass merchandisers nationwide and you can call Gerber (Michigan) at **800/4-GERBER (800/443-7237)** for local stores.

The **Kid Kaper®** towel ($15 to $17) by Leachco is a multi-purpose towel that stays on Charlie, even when he wiggles away after his bath. It fits easily over his head with a ribbed-knit neck and is open on the sides almost like a toga. It's made of thick,

soft cotton terry in assorted colors with adorable satin appliques. Designed for ages four months and up, the towel can be used as a versatile cover-up for arts and crafts, for the beach and at meal or snack time. You can get this wonderful towel through select J.C. Penney stores and One Step Ahead (Illinois) at **800/274-8440** or call Leachco (Oklahoma) at **800/525-1050** for local stores or to order direct.

PERSONAL CARE PRODUCTS

I've discovered a number of outstanding personal care products for Charlie (and in many cases for myself as well).

The first soap I ever used on Charlie is called appropriately **Babycakes®** ($2.50 to $2.75) by Only Natural. It's a gentle soap

made with natural ingredients (which are printed on the box) that are good for a baby's skin and for the environment. It lathers nicely, rinses off easily and holds its shape, never cracking. I've also used Only Natural's **Camomile** soap on Charlie. Call

Only Natural (Massachusetts) at **508/745-9766** for local natural food stores or to order direct.

The first shampoo I used on Charlie was **Tom's of Maine Natural Baby Shampoo.** Created in 1975, this was the first natural baby shampoo on the market. It is made from the highest quality natural ingredients and is packaged in recycled and recyclable bottles (made from recycled milk jugs). I love the delicate honeysuckle scent of this shampoo, too, and it rinses easily. It's available nationally at over 7,000 health food stores and in over 20,000 food and drug stores on the east and west coasts.

For Charlie's skin, we've used three products. Ever since Charlie was a tiny infant, we've really liked **Un-Petroleum Jelly®**

(about $3 for a four-ounce jar) by Autumn Harp, which looks much like petroleum jelly, though it feels less greasy, is more readily absorbed into the skin and uses natural, petroleum-free ingredients. I've used it on Charlie's face when it becomes red from drooling or from the elements and found it to be very healing. You can also use it as a moisture barrier in diapering. Available in health food stores and drug stores, it comes packaged with a free tube of Un-Petroleum® Lip Balm for Mom or Dad. Call Autumn Harp (Vermont) **802/453-4807** for a local distributor.

I've just started testing **Nature's Second Skin** (about $13) by Lansinoh Laboratories, which is a patented formulation of pure Lansinoh (see Chapter 2, page 23) plus 10 percent ultra purified

lanolin oil for ease of application to larger body areas. Product testing by the manufacturer has shown this product to be useful for healing diaper rash, cradle cap, dry skin and even skinned knees. It's available through the La Leche League International Catalog (Illinois) at **708/451-1891** or call Lansinoh Laboratories (Tennessee) at **800/292-4794** for the name of a local drug store or health food store.

For a general moisturizer that applies easily, I like Healthy Times **Baby Cream With Orchid Oil** (about $3.60). It's hypoallergenic and has a natural baby scent. Healthy Times products are available at most health food stores in the U.S. and Canada and some grocery stores. You can call Healthy Times (California) directly at **619/464-1622** if you have any difficulty obtaining a product.

Trimming Charlie's finger nails, especially when he was an infant, has been particularly challenging. I generally do it after he's fallen asleep. I use **The First Years Baby Scissors** (No. 3201, about $3.35), which have curved, rustproof, stainless steel blades with special rounded tips and come in a convenient storage pouch. For those remaining rough edges that can scratch tender skin and snag clothing, emery boards for babies are handy (Revlon makes them). For store locations, call The First Years/ Kiddie Products, Inc. (Massachusetts) at **800/533-6708**.

DENTAL CARE

The importance of first cleaning your baby's gums and then the teeth later on can't be overemphasized. I've found some products that can make it easier.

Our family dentist, Dr. Sadie Mestman, (who is herself a mother with a toddler), advised me very early on to get a wonderful little patented device called the **Infa-Dent® Finger Toothbrush and Gum Massager** (about $2) by Nu-Tec. It slips

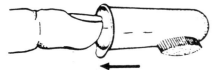

on your finger, is easy to use and gently removes plaque and soothes sore gums. The suggested age range is birth to three years but I was only able to use it with Charlie up until about one year (when he started to bite down on my finger I switched to a toothbrush). Call Nu-Tec (California) at **619/720-2223** for a local store or to order direct.

I have used several different toothbrushes with Charlie. I really like the **MagMag Toothbrush System** (about $8), which includes three oral training accessories to clean and sooth gums and first teeth. The system is available through The Right Start Catalog (California) at **800/526-5220**, One Step Ahead (Illinois) at **800/274-8440** or call Marshall Baby Products (Illinois) at **800/634-4350** for a store in your area.

The First Years My Own Toothbrush, No. 3210 (about $2.10) has a safety shield that prevents the toothbrush from going in too far. For store locations, call The First Years (Kiddie Products, Inc.) at **800/533-6708** (Massachusetts).

Although toddlers want to brush by themselves, Dr. Mestman recommends that parents actively help with brushing up until about seven years of age. "Young children really don't have the motor coordination to do a thorough job," she says, "and so you have to take control over it."

She suggests a place other than the bathroom for brushing where you can easily distract your toddler from resisting. Putting on a video or telling a story can work. Letting your toddler brush by himself or herself after you're done brushing their teeth is another possibility. Try reading children's books on brushing and the dentist such as *Mr. Rogers First Experience Books: Going to the Dentist* (Putnam Publishing, about $6). To speed up the process, Dr. Mestman also recommends using an **electric toothbrush** (about $70) which can to speed up the process to a quick but thorough 30-second job.

From about 1½ to six years of age, Dr. Mestman recommends using a tiny amount of fluoridated toothpaste, no more than the size of a small pea. My favorite toothpaste for Charlie is **Tom's of Maine Natural Toothpaste for Children** that comes in "Out-

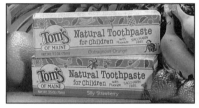

rageous Orange" and "Silly Strawberry." It's the first and only natural toothpaste with fluoride that is made especially for kids. (I've been using the adult Tom's toothpaste for years but I like these new ones even better.) See page 45 for availability of Tom's of Maine products.

BATH TOYS

Bath time is a wonderful play time because water is such an exciting medium to explore. There are a number of toys that have helped Charlie explore this medium, develop his small motor coordination and have put him more at ease with bathing and shampooing (which he hasn't always been wild about).

Charlie loves two Fisher-Price® toys from their Kiddicraft®

line. **Play Buckets** (No. 5606, about $7) have provided lots of fun and include three colorful buckets with friendly faces that nest neatly together. One sprinkles, one has a spout and one pours out of its "mouth." You could also use them for sand play. The suggested age range is 1 to 5 years.

Captain Stack (No. 5677, about $8) is a five-piece take-apart toy consisting of a life ring and three boats, including a sailboat and a captain who whistles when he's pushed in the water. The suggested ages are one to three. Check with Toys R Us, Wal-

Mart, K-Mart and Target or call Fisher-Price (New York) at **800/432-KIDS (800/432-5437)** for a store near you.

Charlie continues to enjoy his **Toddle Tots® Noah's Ark** (No. 0011, $19 to $23) by Little Tikes, which is shown below "on land." As the brochure copy aptly states, this ark "will withstand 40 days and 40 nights in the bathtub." For ages one to five, the ark includes Noah, his wife, and eight chunky animals—two elephants, two giraffes, two sheep and two chickens. Noah, his wife and the chickens do best in the ark as they can get a little waterlogged if they take too long a dip in the bathtub water. Check major retailers and the J.C. Penney catalog or call Little Tikes (Ohio) at **800/321-0183** for local stores.

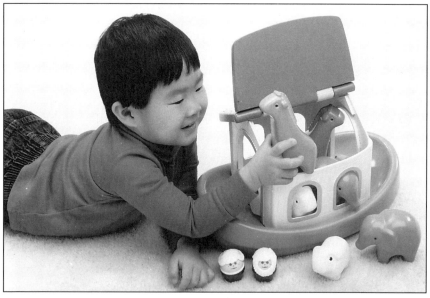

The **First Years Stack'em Up Cups** (No. 2311, about $7.20) are ten colored, numbered, stacking and nesting cups that are great in the bathtub—they even float! They're for ages nine months and up. For store locations, call The First Years/Kiddie Products, Inc. (Massachusetts) at **800/533-6708**.

We participated in the **Child Development Toys Program** from Parents® Magazine, which is a toy club, similar to a book club, that I discuss more fully in Chapter 9 (pages 93-94). Two favorites were bath toys (which are also available through some retail stores). Charlie has enjoyed his **Ship Shape Village** (about $7.50 when purchased through the program), which consists of a simple floating dock and boat, a captain and a sailor, and

Bathtime Water Works (about $11), which comes with a floating raft with different sprinkling holes and three water toys—two cups and a squirter.

Finally, going through the Playskool catalog, I saw a couple of bath toys that look like fun. Both attach to tub walls with suction cups. The **Busy Splash 'n Play**™ (No. 5213, about $8.80) has a scooper boat, water tap, paddle wheel, squirter and water strainer. The **Busy Bubble Maker**™ (No. 5225, about $18.90) features a bubble-making lighthouse, a net to catch bubbles, a turtle to sprinkle water, a spinning paddle wheel and a floating boat.

6

Indoors at Its Best

Growing babies spend many hours indoors, especially those who live in places with extreme temperatures. The more time they spend indoors, the greater the challenges in keeping them safe, comfortable and stimulated. In this chapter you'll see some innovative products for baby proofing, storing baby's things, indoor seating (for sitting, playing and napping) and products for comforting your baby during mishaps or illness.

BABY PROOFING PRODUCTS
The trick to baby proofing is creating the safest physical environment for your baby—knowing how to spot possible dangers and to eliminate those dangers well before your baby is old enough to discover them.

I've also found it often takes some real creativity and ingenuity to solve baby proofing problems especially if you can't find the right products for your problems. And when you're already running low on energy, who has time to spend countless hours researching and testing products?

To save you time, however, I want to share with you some of the best baby proofing products (and sources of products) our family uses. This is by no means a comprehensive list because baby proofing is a highly individual matter. Therefore, I

50

enthusiastically recommend you get a copy of *The Perfectly Safe® Home* (about $10) by Jeanne Miller (published by Simon & Schuster), which is indeed quite comprehensive. I read this wonderful book from cover to cover and continue to refer to it. With over 284 illustrated pages, this book covers in depth such important topics as safety in every room of your home, how to be safe outdoors and on the road, which specific safety devices you may need and how to select safe toys by age group. It's thoroughly researched and so well-organized that you can find information quickly.

Next, get a copy of the **Perfectly Safe Catalog** (Ohio) by calling **800/837-KIDS (800/837-5437)**. This catalog features baby proofing products, most of which have been tested by their advisory board. Just going carefully through this catalog is a real education about all of the possible hidden dangers lurking in your baby's environment. Many of the items in this section of my book are available through this catalog.

Sharp edges and corners of furniture are real hazards for standing, cruising or walking babies. I found the plastic corners with the self-adhesive tape didn't work at all. Once my son discovered them, he thought they were excellent teethers! I was afraid that they would come loose and wind up in his mouth or throat. So I ended up removing them and discovered a great product called **Toddler Shield** by OFNA Baby Products.

Toddler Shield hugs and cushions the edges and corners of  coffee, dining and end tables. We use Toddler Shield on our dining room table. It's designed for tables with overhanging edges (it won't work on a table whose legs are flush with the table edge). It's easy to install and comes in three sizes: 1) 60-140 inches for end tables and small coffee tables (Model TS-1140-01, about $30); 2) 93-192 inches for standard coffee tables (TS-1001-01, about $40); and 3) 140-270 inches for larger dining tables and custom coffee tables (TS-1270-01, about $60). You can order direct from OFNA Baby Products (California) at **714/586-2910** or through the **Perfectly Safe Catalog** (Ohio) by calling **800/837-5437**.

I spent a lot of time researching a safe enclosure that was much bigger than a play pen (now euphemistically called "a play yard"), was portable and could be used for babies through toddlers (although preferably for only very short periods of time since it's better for their development to be in a more open environment). **Superyard** (No. 8634, about $65) by North States Industries was the answer.

Superyard is JPMA certified in the "enclosures" category and is extremely versatile. It can be increased or decreased in size by removing or adding two panels at a time. I bought the two-panel extension kit (about $23) to increase the size from 18.5 square feet to 34.4 square feet. It's portable and can be used inside or out.

We have used and enjoyed Superyard in many ways. At one time we had it in our bedroom, where Charlie would play in the early morning hours while we tried to get in a few more winks (while watching him out of the corner of one eye). It's now in the living room and is positioned to block off the area next to the television. We once took it to a party when Charlie was standing but not yet walking and many of the older kids there had so much fun getting right in there with him. I, too, can easily climb over and play right alongside Charlie. You can also open up Superyard at any one of the panels, which open like a gate.

Made of durable polypropylene plastic resin, it's easily cleaned with soap and water and can even be hosed off. For new crawlers, you may want to cushion some of the hard edges with soft items such as towels or stuffed animals. Call North States at **612/541-9101** for local stores or order through the Perfectly Safe Catalog (Ohio) at **800/837-KIDS (800/837-5437)**, The Right Start Catalog (California) at **800/548-8531** or One Step Ahead (Illinois) at **800/274-8440**.

I searched long and hard for an easy-to-use and easy-to-install security gate to keep Charlie out of certain rooms. I am happy with the **Gerry® Walk-Thru Gate** (No. 545, about $33). It's a spring-loaded pressure gate that installs without drilling and

hardware (although you do have to carefully read and follow the instructions). It swings completely open in both directions for walk-through convenience and has a one-hand release for adults. I find you do have to occasionally readjust it because some slipping occurs with frequent use. Adapting to base-boards and uneven openings, the gate ex-pands from 28 to 39 inches wide and is 27 inches high. It's also useful as a barrier for pets. Call Gerry (Colorado) at **800/525-2472** for a location in your area.

You're going to also want to have locks and latches for furniture, appliances and even your VCR. **Video Halt** (about $13) is a unique, universal lock for front loading VCRs that lets you play a video cassette and at the same time lock your VCR to protect toddlers from exploring with fingers and objects. Unlike other VCR devices, this one always stays in place and comes with two keys (the manufacturer recommends you keep one on your key chain). It's available from The Right Start Catalog (California) at **800/548-8531** or for other distributors call Video Halt (New York) at **518/237-5246**.

Victor's Latch (about $2.50) is a new, safety, appliance latch made of high grade, polycarbonate plastic (that's virtually un-

breakable) for refrigerators, dryers and metal cabinets. We use it and have found that it works so much better than those Velcro® closure straps that often come loose. For availability of this patented latch that's made in the U.S., contact Victor's Latch (New York) at **516/668-9249.**

For our oven we use the **Safety 1st® Oven Lock** (No. 241, about $2), which is a heat resistant latch that secures the door in a closed position until you're ready to open it with a squeeze. We use the handy **Safety 1st Cabinet Slide Lock** (No. 110N, about $1.40), 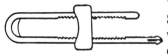 which is shown here, all over the house on our cabinet doors that have knobs. Both are easy to use. For store locations call Safety 1st (Massachusetts) at **800/962-7233.**

We also use **The First Years Cabinet Safety Latch** (No. 3232, 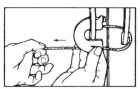 about $1.90), which is about 1½ inches longer, has a rounded shape and will fit a wider range of cabinet knobs. I like that the operating directions are printed right on this latch for handy reference. The strap loops through or around most side-by-side cabinet door handles. You can also trim off the excess strap with a scissors for extra safety and a neater appearance.

The First Years Nightlight with Socket Cover (No. 3517, about  $9.50) combines photosensitive nighttime lighting needs with outlet protection (when an outlet's not being used with a plug). This is a great night light in the bathroom, which is where we've been using it. You just plug the product in the top socket of an outlet—the light's on top and the bottom portion opens to accept a plug or closes securely when not in use. Make sure you have a single screw outlet plate. For store locations, call The First Years/Kiddie Products, Inc. (Massachusetts) at **800/533-6708.**

Gerber makes two handy baby proofing devices we use on doors. Their **Door Knob Cover With Lock Guard** (No. 76382, about $2.70) helps keep your baby or toddler from off-limit 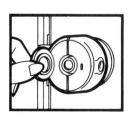 rooms. It's fairly easy to install and remove and is easy for an adult to turn a knob with the cover in place. It also features a "Lock Guard" device (shown in the picture) that works on a knob with a central lock. When closed, this device prevents toddlers from locking themselves in a bathroom or other room. An adult, however, can snap open the lock guard to operate a central lock.

Gerber's pair of **Flexible Door Stops** (No. 76191, about $1.70)

are an easy way to prevent toddlers from closing doors on little fingers. Made of a soft, non-mar rubber, these door stops won't harm doors and are easy to use. By changing the location of the stop, you can change how much the doors close. Call Gerber (Michigan) at **800/4-GERBER (800/443-7237)** to find where their products are sold.

Here's a little inexpensive item I use to train baby sitters. It's the **Safety 1st Small Object Tester** (No. 126, about $1) and is

specifically designed to test the safety of toys and other items for children under three years old by clearly showing those that are too small and would present a choking hazard. A handy training tool, it visually makes the point about keeping small objects away from babies and toddlers. You should, of course, emphasize to baby sitters that they use their own best judgment and remove all small questionable objects (even those that "pass" this tester). The tester conforms to Consumer Product Safety Commission regulations. For store locations call Safety 1st (Massachusetts) at **800/962-7233**.

Be on the lookout for the new **Playskool® Baby Safe-Store Pail™** (about $8), which features a patented lock closure that

keeps the lid shut on harmful household products. It looks ideal for storing hazardous household chemicals, cleaners and other harmful compounds. Important poison control numbers are listed on the 2½-gallon pail itself. For availability of this new product, call Playskool (Rhode Island) at **401/431-TOYS (401/431-8697)**.

STORAGE ORGANIZERS

If you had home organization challenges before your baby, just wait until you're inundated with toys and clothing!

You're going to need to take control by having good organizational systems. In my consulting business, Positively Organized! (which is *not* to be confused with *compulsively* organized), I teach clients that any good system has two parts: the right tools and the right habits.

The right habits include having routines for daily cleanup and for periodic (at least several times a year) cleaning out sessions, in which you either store or give away toys and clothing. It's going to take some real work to manage all this stuff because unfortunately, your baby's room isn't a self-cleaning oven. Although it will be a while before your toddler can help significantly, actively begin some basic organizational training at the first signs of readiness (which often occur as early as 18 months and more typically from 24 to 36 months.)

The right organizational habits also need the right tools—storage organizers that are accessible and easy to use. My first advice as an organization expert is stay away from big toy chests and "dump-em-in" bins. Choose instead book and toy shelves and durable *stacking* boxes and bins. Rubbermaid makes a wonderful selection of boxes and bins. We use their **Keepers™ Clear Boxes** shown here (No. 2223, 23 by 16¾ by 9 inches, about $15) and their **Keepers™ Snap Cases** (No. 2281, 14 by 7¾ by 4½ inches, about $5). Lightly tinted in six attractive colors—blue, pink, green, lilac, dusty plum and misty spruce—they are clear enough to see what you're storing.

Keepers Stacking Bins (No. 3008, 18 by 13¼ by 8¾ inches high, about $7 each) stack up just about anywhere for space-saving, open storage. These sturdy, plastic bins nest and stack

and come in red, white, blue and yellow. If you want a portable 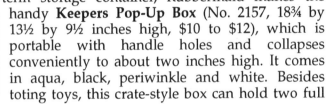three-bin unit with strong, swivel casters, check out their **Cart Wheels™ Bin Cart** (No. 2428, about $25), which comes in white, periwinkle or a primary combination. (You can also break down the bins on this modular cart to use them separately.)

If you want clear but closed storage with clear front doors, consider **Keepers Window Bins** (No. 2704 to 2706, in small, medium and large sizes, about $10 to $18). They stack and come in slate blue or primary colors.

For a short-term storage container, Rubbermaid makes the 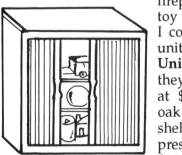handy **Keepers Pop-Up Box** (No. 2157, 18¾ by 13½ by 9½ inches high, $10 to $12), which is portable with handle holes and collapses conveniently to about two inches high. It comes in aqua, black, periwinkle and white. Besides toting toys, this crate-style box can hold two full grocery bags.

For long-term storage that is durable, moisture resistent and lockable, look at Rubbermaid's **Keepers Totelocker** (No. 2156, 32 by 17¼ by 13 inches, about $40) and **Totelocker Jr.** (No. 2155, 18 by 18 by 16½ inches, about $25). They come in slate blue or a combination of purple and aqua. Rubbermaid products are available in mass merchandise, discount and hardware/home center stores or call Rubbermaid (Ohio) at **216/264-6464** for store locations or to order direct. Ask for consumer service.

Currently much of our toy storage resides in a wonderful toy cabinet I designed that sits in our living/family room. I had looked all over for a deep cabinet (one at least 24 inches deep) with tambour sliding doors that was big enough to block our fireplace (it was to do double duty for toy storage and for baby proofing). When I couldn't find it, I went to a local wall unit furniture store named **Carl's Wall Units** in Los Angeles and discovered they could have it custom made for me at $489. It's a quality piece with solid oak frame and doors and two adjustable shelves and sides made of oak veneer on prescore wood. I selected an oiled oak finish (which I felt would be more practical with Charlie) but other finishes are available. The tambour doors slide closed (so we don't have to constantly look at the toys). You can order a custom or stock piece from Carl's (**310/207-9964**), which will ship nationwide (the customer pays for shipping). Ask for Carl Greeson.

Diplomat Juvenile Corp. provides some clever space-saving solutions for storage of stuffed animals and dolls with their **Rosie's Babies**™ line of toy hammocks that hang on a wall. The **Super Size Toy Hammock** (No. 805, about $10) is over six feet long and the **Toy Hammock With Wall Hanging** (No. 803, about $25) includes a soft sculpture wall hanging of a hot air balloon (in either primary or pastel colors). Five other wall hanging styles are available, too—heart, baseball, football, train and balloons. Hardware isn't included. You can call Diplomat Juvenile Corp. in New York at **800/247-9063** for a store near you.

To maximize our shortage of closet space, we use the modular **Selfix® Cubby Cubes** (No. 7013, about $20), which comes with

four plastic cubes and a clothes rod. The cubes are red and the hardware is yellow and blue. The assembly requires no tools but is a little time-consuming. (You'll also want to do it away from your baby or toddler because there are many small parts.) The directions on the package are clear. You can also buy three cubes without the rod—**Kids Cubes** (No. 7004, about $15). Because the cubes and their components are modular, you can create any number of different designs. All Selfix Tidy Kids products are U.S.-made and beside cubes, consist of an entire line of juvenile organizers in primary colors, including hangers, a closet extender kit and self-stick or screw-installation shelves, hooks and racks. Products are available at Target and Toys R Us as well as through The Right Start Catalog (California) at **800/548-8531** where I first saw it, and the J.C. Penney and Spiegel catalogs. Call Selfix (Illinois) at **800/327-3534** for local stores.

INDOOR SEATING
FOR SITTING, PLAYING AND NAPPING

I never knew how much effort it would take for Charlie just to learn how to sit. Fortunately, there are some wonderful products to make this process easier.

Next time I would use **Snuggle-Up™** (about $17) by Leachco  for my newborn infant. This is a soft yet firm polyester fiberfill multi-position pillow that provides maximum head and body support in an infant seat, swing or stroller. Uniquely placed Velcro® tabs let you easily change the versatile Snuggle-Up into six different positions that are shown in the helpful instruction sheet. Made in the U.S., it's available through children's specialty stores, select J.C. Penney stores or call Leachco (Oklahoma) at **800/525-1050** for local stores or to order direct.

Boppy "The Pillow Pal" ($30 to $38) by Camp Kazoo would have been a great help to Charlie when he was learning to sit and balance. Designed by a mom with the help of a day care center, Boppy is an award-winning (one of JPMA's best new 1990 products) multi-use pillow that is 100 percent cotton, polyester filled and machine washable. Boppy's cozy crescent shape gives infants and babies a comfy and secure place to lie while awake. Also great for change of pace floor play, nonsitting babies can be placed on either their chest or back on Boppy for different angles to observe their environment or play with toys. And when babies are learning to sit, Boppy props them upright and cushions them if they fall to the side. Distributed by 800 retail stores nationwide, the U.S.-made Boppy is also available through The Right Start Catalog (California) at **800/548-8531** and One Step Ahead (Illinois) at **800/274-8440**.

 Camp Kazoo has two other Boppy products. The **Boppy Lay and Play** ($20 to $30) is ideal for babies three to six months when they love to play on their tummies. Like the Boppy pillow, it allows babies to position themselves comfortably on their chests and play with toys spread before them but it also has a quilt-like extension upon which

they can lie while awake. You can also use the Boppy Lay and Play as a changing pad up to about 12 months. Resting on the pillow, babies have a better view than lying flat. It's distributed by 800 stores and it's also available through One Step Ahead (Illinois) at **800/274-8440** and the Hand in Hand catalog (Maine) at **800/543-4343**.

If toddlers go to day care, chances are good they'll nap. Camp Kazoo's **The Happy Napper** ($30 to $40) is designed to attach

 easily to standard mats provided by day care centers to provide a comfortable place to nap. It has a Boppy-shape pillow built in. Distributed by 800 stores, it's also available through One Step Ahead (Illinois) at **800/274-8440** and the Lands End catalog (Wisconsin) at **800/356-4444**.

In Chapter 1 I talked about the Evenflo Swing for newborns. Although you can continue to use this swing when your infant is no longer a newborn, you may also want to have a more conventional, battery-operated swing that gives your baby a different view of the world. I would select one that has at least two features: a combination seat/carrier (which can be easily removed from the swing for use as a baby carrier) and a pivoting, easy-to-open, lift-off tray that makes it easier to get your baby into the swing. (Here are some tips for using such a tray: pull the swing forward; lift the tray up and over so that it rests propped against a swing leg, making the seat stationary; and then put your baby in the seat.)

I would get either the **Graco Battery-Powered Carrier/Rocker Swing** (No. 1301, about $100) or the **Century® Kanga-Rocka-Roo® Plus** (No. 12-489, about $71), which is shown here. Both

 offer a semi-recline rocking position, which should probably be fine for your newborn (although check with your pediatrician to make sure). You may also want to provide some additional head support with the Snuggle-Up, for example (see page 59). Both have seats that can be removed and used as multiple-position carriers. The Century Kanga-Rocka-Roo Plus has a storage pouch on the back of the swing and also has detachable links and toys. Call Century (Ohio) at **800/837-4044** and Graco (Pennsylvania) at **215/286-5951** for local store names.

Once you have a toddler who's not only sitting but involved in all kinds of activities, you'll ideally want to have a variety of

equipment on hand indoors, especially for those days with very cold or hot weather. Although many of these equipment pieces can also be used outdoors, we have found them ideal for indoor seating and play.

A rocking horse is a good basic piece and Charlie continues to enjoy his **Little Tikes® Rocking Horse** (No. 4017, $20 to $25). With a high seat back, an easy-to-hold handle, and a low center of gravity, this stable rocking horse lets toddlers ages one to three rock with feet on or off the floor. And there's no assembly required. Little Tikes products are at all major retail chain stores, toy discounters and small toy stores as well as the J.C. Penney catalog. You can call Little Tikes (Ohio) at **800/321-0183** for local retailers.

Today's Kids makes three items Charlie enjoys all of which combine sitting with activities. The multiple award-winning **Activity Rocker™** (No. 390, about $35) by Today's Kids is designed as baby's first sit up activity toy and comes with a safety belt as well as an adjustable seat that lets this rocker grow with your baby. For ages eight months to 2½ years (although I think its better suited at the lower end), the rocker has nine sight and sound activities. The action console has a confetti-filled clicking push dome, a pop-open door with peek-a-boo mirror inside, an echo phone, a twisting key that doubles as a teether, a spinning roller with colorful graphics, a three-position ratchet-sound gear shift and two hand-holds for vigorous rocking. The Activity Rocker won awards from JPMA (1990) and Oppenheim Toy Portfolio (1991).

I like Today's Kids' **Play Table** (No. 260NC, about $32) because it's sized small enough for a young toddler (the age range is 1½ to seven years) and doesn't take up a lot of space. I also like the red top, which is a practical color. It's perfect for year-round, indoor-outdoor activities.

Today's Kids **Alpha Desk™** (No. 925, about $40), shown at left, is a perfect first desk, designed specifically for kids two and older. It has 48 large letters and numbers that attach safely without magnets to the bristle-back surface underneath the desk top. It also features a two-position adjustable desk top, removable accessory tray, wipe-off marker surface, desk top pencil slot and a large storage area. Today's Kids products, most of which are completely made in the U.S., are available at Toys R Us, K-Mart, Target and Service Merchandise or call Today's Kids (Arkansas) at **800/258-TOYS (800/258-8697)** for a store near you.

With regard to *your* seating, if you use a rocking chair, Sandbox Industries makes several handy accessories. **Rock-R-Roll**™ (No. 1260, about $13), ties to the back of the chair and provides a soft cushion for your head. **Rock-R-Roll With Pockets** (No. 1270, about $21), ties to the arm of the chair for gentle arm support and provides convenient storage for baby bottles and other baby needs. If you have a glider rocker, Sandbox also makes cushioned slipcovers. These products are available through Bellini and USA Baby stores throughout the U.S. or call Sandbox (New Jersey) at **800/451-6636** for catalog or local store names.

TAKING THE STRAIN OUT OF PAIN
When I'm indoors with Charlie helping him nurse a cold, bring down a fever or tend to a bump, I've found several products that make it easier on both him and me.

Taking a baby's temperature has to be one of a parent's worst nightmares. I gave up on taking a rectal temperature long ago and switched over to "axillary" (underarm), which isn't very

accurate and still not easy or fast enough. But I've just found an incredible product that literally takes a few seconds. The **Thermoscan HM-1** (about $120) is an infrared tympanic (ear) thermometer that measures the infrared heat generated by the eardrum and surrounding tissue and displays the temperature in one second. Clinically accurate, the Thermoscan HM-1 improves temperature-taking by making it faster, safer, cleaner and easier. It comes with helpful instructions, a storage case (which has a quick-reference/error message guide), a battery and eight reusable probe covers. You can specify either oral or rectal equivalent temperatures. Be sure to talk with your pediatrician about this exciting new thermometer. Thermoscan is available at department stores nationwide (call **800/EAR-SCAN** or **800/327-7226**) or order through The Right Start Catalog (California) at **800/548-8531** or The Sharper Image (California) at **800/344-4444**.

For bumps and bruises we keep a couple of items handy in the freezer. The **Safety 1st N'ICE BEAR** (No. 143, about $2.50) is a reusable, non-toxic cold pack that is filled with water. It's easy for a toddler to hold. For store locations call Safety 1st (Massachusetts) at **1/800/962-7233**.

The **BumpBag™** from American Baby Concepts ($6 to $6.50) is a soft, flexible, specially filled canvas bag that gets cold but prevents freezer burn. It's non-toxic and even machine-washable. Call **800/537-7181** (Iowa) for a store near you.

MISCELLANY
Here's a product that belongs in this chapter but not under the previous headings.

Sleeper Keeper™ (about $30 for a twin size) is the first and only custom sheet designed to keep children covered throughout the night. It's really two sheets in one: a bottom, fitted sheet and a top sheet that's sewn at the foot portion with air pockets on each side and attached with 18 feet of Velcro® and snap closures. Designed by a mom, Sleeper Keeper is machine washer/dryer safe and helps making the bed a snap. Charlie tested out the twin size on his toddler bed (the toddler size Sleeper Keeper isn't available as of this writing) and discovered it was great. Two specially sewn pleats provide extra room as Charlie tosses and turns through the night. You can order this new product direct from Sleeper Keeper by sending $29.95 plus $3 for shipping to Sleeper Keeper, PO Box 10021, Newport Beach, CA 92660. The phone is **714/262-1474**.

7

The Best
On-the-Go Products

Chances are, you'll be out and about with your baby almost as much as you're indoors, or at least it seems that way. And for many people, it takes almost as much time and energy getting ready to go out as the outing itself. That's why it's important to have great on-the-go products on hand to streamline the process as much as possible and save yourself wasted energy. Having travel checklists for different types of outings is essential, too. I keep one posted for daily outings right on the front door near the diaper bag.

In this chapter you'll see my picks for the best strollers and accessories, diaper bags and other totes, car travel products, mealtime items, products for changing time, "out in public" helpers and overnight items. (See also Chapter 10, pages 114-118, for traveling toys and Chapter 11 for tapes and books, which also make great traveling companions.)

STROLLERS
After having used and tested many, many strollers, I have identified the types of strollers I like, the features that are most important to me in a stroller and several models I specifically recommend.

There are five types of strollers that exist in the marketplace today. The **carriage** is for newborns and very young babies up to four months or so. It provides a nice flat sleeping area but because it's used for such a short period of time and because other strollers also provide a flat sleeping area, I don't recommend this type of stroller.

The **carriage stroller**, also called a **convertible stroller**, combines the flat sleeping area of a carriage with the features of a stroller, including an adjustable seat back. I recommend this versatile stroller, which you can use from birth for several years.

The **umbrella stroller** (so named because of its umbrella-like handles) is a very lightweight travel stroller that's handy but usually has very few features and often is lacking in durability.

A new stroller called the **convenience stroller** has emerged and is a cross between the carriage stroller and umbrella stroller. It's lightweight like an umbrella stroller, usually ten pounds or less, but offers more carriage stroller features. For example, many convenience strollers offer several seat positions, including a reclining one, and come with a basket underneath the seat. I like the concept behind the convenience stroller, even though it doesn't yet have all the features I want. This is definitely a stroller to watch develop over the next several years.

Finally, if you have two young children, you'll want a **double stroller**, sometimes called a **twin stroller**. I prefer the tandem style to the side by side models, which are difficult to maneuver on the street and through doorways.

I look for five features in a stroller. First, it has to be a safe, quality stroller and preferably one that is JPMA-certified (see page 140 on JPMA certification).

Second, it has to be both lightweight (no more than about 13 pounds) and have a ratcheting hood and/or a reversible handle. Because I live in very sunny California, a ratcheting hood that moves back and forth and far enough forward to block out the sun from a baby's eyes and face, is essential for me. A "reversible handle" can let you switch directions, too, but it's too much trouble to use for this purpose. (It is, however, a nice feature for a newborn stroller because it lets you face your baby so you can keep a better eye on him or her.) It's much easier to just quickly move a ratcheting hood down, but very few strollers have what I deem to be this essential feature. (See also page 86 in Chapter 8, which describes how Baby Optics sunglasses and the Flap Happy hat can also help with sun protection.)

Third, it should be easy to operate, in terms of opening and closing, as well as "road handling." Fourth, a large roomy basket underneath is a very nice plus. Fifth, your stroller should ideally be usable from birth through the toddler years.

I have found one stroller that comes closest to meeting all my criteria. It's the **Peg Perego Amico**, (No. 15-00-010, about $189).

It weighs about 13 pounds and the manufacturer says can fit into an overhead storage on a plane (of course, always check with the airline first as you should do for any stroller). Besides having a large, ratcheting hood, this stroller has an optional cover for a baby's legs that will provide extra special protection in inclement weather. While there is no reversible handle, there is a clear vinyl opening in the waterproof hood to keep an eye on baby. This JPMA-certified stroller opens and closes easily and handles very smoothly. It has three seating positions, including full recline, so a baby can nap in a comfortable position. The quilted upholstery can be completely removed and washed. The basket could be bigger but can be remedied with the **Tag-Along Stroll-A-Bag** discussed on page 69. The only negative about the Amico is that when it has been closed and is self-standing, the cloth covered footrest is only an inch or so off the ground so you have to be careful to set it down on a flat, reasonably clean surface (or don't set it down at all). I am using the Amico with Charlie and we both really enjoy it.

If you have twins or two very young children, Peg Perego makes several twin strollers. The one I'd choose, based on re-

search but not testing, is the **Tender** (No. 15-19-200, about $309). It's made of lightweight aluminum and is supposed to fold easily and compactly. The backrest in each seat of this tandem stroller will fully recline and each seat has its own complete hood for weather protection. The split footrest on the rear seat allows a sleepy child to lie flat in a fully enclosed carriage-like setting. And both hoods ratchet back and forth. For a distributor near you, call Peg Perego U.S.A. (Indiana) at **219/484-3093**.

A very lightweight **convenience stroller** may be nice to have for traveling. Unfortunately, there isn't one that has a ratcheting hood. It is, however, more durable with more features than an "umbrella stroller." I'd get either the **Aprica Newborn LX** (about $370), which weighs 10 pounds, or the Aprica **CitiMini** (about

$276), which weighs only seven pounds. I tested the new Newborn LX (which is shown here in upright and reclining positions) and found it to be very easy to use with a special "one touch" operation that lets you literally open and close the stroller with one hand (the CitiMini also has this feature). The Newborn LX, however, has three reclining positions, up to 170 degrees, and includes a leg extension, whereas the CitiMini only has one reclining position at 140 degrees and no leg extension. Both of these should fit in most airplane overhead compartments (again, check with the airline). Both these JPMA certi-fied strollers have medium size mesh baskets, stand when folded, have removable safety bars and have locking wheels. Call Aprica USA (California) at **714/634-0402** for names of local stores.

STROLLER ACCESSORIES THAT ARE NECESSITIES

Because Charlie was a June baby, I enjoyed an easy-to-use

product called **Rosie's Babies™ Stroller Netting** by Diplomat (No. 704, about $4) to keep insects such as flies and mosquitos out of my newborn's stroller. Made of 100 per-cent fine mesh, see-through nylon, it's ma-chine washer and dryer safe. Diplomat also makes netting to fit carriages (shown here), playpens, crib, portable cribs and portable play yards. You can call Diplomat Juvenile Corp. in New York at **800/247-9063** for a store near you.

Prince Lionheart makes several handy stroller accessories. Their **LOVE BUG™** (No. 6701, $12 to $13) repels mosquitoes by electronically duplicating the tone of the dragonfly's wingbeat (mosquitoes *hate* dragon-flies!) The safe, low-level tone is barely audible to humans. A flashing red light shows that the Love Bug is working. Effective within a 20- to 30-foot radius, the Love Bug can be clipped onto a stroller (or play yard, too).

Prince Lionheart's **STROLLER SHIELD** (No. 6401, $11 to $12) is a clear vinyl cover that protects a baby from rain, wind and snow. It has a fitted front boot, fastening tabs and generous mesh fabric windows for ventilation.

Be on the lookout for their **STROLLER ACCESSORY BAR** (No. 6500, about $17), which has four hook hangers (two that move) plus a versatile drink holder that expands to fit virtually any size beverage container. The drink holder is also "gimballed," meaning it keeps drinks level even if the stroller is at an angle. I saw a prototype for this item that fits full-size (not umbrella) strollers. Call Prince Lionheart at **800/544-1132** (805/922-2250 in California) for a local store or to mail order these products, which are made in the U.S.

Be on the lookout, too, for the new **Playskool® Baby Stroller Tray** (about $9), which was promoted at the JPMA show I

attended. The tray attaches to a carriage stroller and has three recessed areas for small toys, bottles, cups or snacks. The tray stays attached even when the stroller is folded and is dishwasher safe. For availability of this new item, call Playskool (Rhode Island) at **401/431-TOYS (401/431-8697)**.

To attach items within Charlie's reach but prevent him from throwing them to the ground, we've used three items. They have saved us from bending over hundreds of times to retrieve bottles and other items that otherwise would have hit the ground and also required cleaning. **The First Years Attach-A-Toy** (No. 3142, about $2) is a strong, easy-to-fasten strap that holds Charlie's toys and teethers so they won't drop or get lost.

I've used it in his stroller but it's also great with a high chair, shopping cart and car seat. (See also Linky Rinks on page 116 of Chapter 10, which can also be used to hold toys in a stroller.) **The First Years Drink Link™** (No. 1112, about $2.45) with a Velcro® fastener holds a bottle or cup within reach and also attaches to a stroller (as shown here), high chair, shopping cart or car seat. For store locations, call The First Years/Kiddie Products (Massachusetts) at **800/533-**

6708.
Once your baby understands and is able to manipulate Velcro®, you may prefer to use the **Snap & Go® Bottle Rings** by Children On the Go (No. 109, about $4.50). I was thrilled to discover this product, which has an extra-long 18-inch strap in blue and pink and two rings (one for standard bottles and one for nursers).

Children On the Go also makes a 28-inch diameter, flexible **Stroller Umbrella** (No. 602/603, about $17 each) that's perfect for strollers that have little sun protection. Call Children on the Go (Illinois) at **800/537-2684** for catalog and store names or to order direct.

If your stroller basket is small, **Tag-Along Stroll-A-Bag** (No. 1292, about $12.50) by American Baby Concepts is big enough to carry everything from toys to handbags, diaper bags and more, yet its mesh is tight enough to hold coins and other small items. The spring-loaded frame lets you attach this washable, U.S.-made bag in seconds, adjust it to nearly any stroller and hold it open for easy one-handed use. It also can fold up with the stroller. Call **800/537-7181** (Iowa) for a store near you.

If you use an umbrella stroller and want to protect the fabric, Sandbox Industries makes a quilted terry with waterproof lining **Stroller Cover** (No. 1102, $14 to $17) in many solid colors. They also make high quality covers for other strollers (with matching diaper bags), which are not waterproof. Call Sandbox (New Jersey) at **800/451-6636** for a store near you that carries their stroller covers.

Once your baby can sit up, you may encounter a new challenge. If your baby is very active and tries to climb up and out of the stroller, the **Rosie's Babies™ Baby Safety Harness** (No. 420, about $7), could be a great investment. It also works on a high chair or shopping cart. Call Diplomat Juvenile Corp. in New York at **800/247-9063** for a store near you.

DIAPER BAGS AND OTHER TOTES
Above everything else, I look for functional, well-organized bags and totes. I had to look long and hard to find diaper bags that have at least three large compartments, preferably all zippered, to organize clothing, food and diaper items into separate enclosed areas; a few handy smaller pockets; and two bottle pockets. I found two diaper bags I really like plus a third, scaled-down waist bag for quick trips.

The **Babies' Alley® Original Multi-Pocket Nylon Traveler**
(No. 6700/1, about $25) is a patented bag
that is lightweight, dirt resistent and durable
with wipe clean components. It has two
large zippered compartments that I use for
food and clothing, two large outside pockets
with Velcro® closures that I use for diapers
and toys, two handy outside bottle pockets,
a small zippered pocket and a small pocket
with a Velcro® tab. With hand carrying
handles and a shoulder strap, the bag comes
in four pastel colors: blue, gray, mint and
pink. Other features include a removable "Changing Gear Organizer," a padded changing pad and a small waterproof "Dirty Duds
Pocket." Call Babies' Alley (New York) at **212/563-1414** for a local
store or to order direct.

I've just discovered two other wonderful bags by **Aprica®**.
The **Duet Diaper Bag** (about $70) is a quality, mail-pouch style
bag with shoulder straps that has four
extra-roomy compartments (three are zippered, one has a Velcro® tab), two inside
3M Thinsulate® bottle pockets, a changing pad and one small inside zippered
pocket. It's fully lined with heavy-duty
vinyl and has durable zippers. Included are patented clips for
attaching the bag to your stroller. It makes a great overnight or
traveling bag, too; I'm planning to test it out on our next trip.

The **Aprica Tag-Along Belt Bag** (about $20) is a small, con-
venient, hands-free diaper bag with an adjustable waist belt (25
to 36 inches), one 3M Thinsulate® outside bottle pocket and six
other versatile pockets (one is a hidden money/wallet pocket).
All pockets are lined with PVC vinyl that can be
wiped clean. It comes in black with white trim. Call
Aprica USA (California) at **714/634-0402** for local
stores.

If you're a working, breastfeeding mom you'll want to have
tote bags for carrying your gear. The **Cool 'n Carry Tote** for
Nursing Mothers by Ameda/Egnell (No. R12363, about $22) is a
zippered, conservative navy color, lightweight, insulated carrying
case that has room enough for a portable pump plus bottles or
freezer bags. It holds a smaller insulated case with two freezer
packs to keep milk cold up to 16 hours. It also comes with four
freezer bags with a sealing clip and ties. If you're planning to get

the Ameda/Egnell hand pump as described on page 21 of Chapter 2, you can save money by getting the **Cool 'n Carry™ Pump 'n Save System** (No. R12360, about $40) shown here, which combines the tote with the pump. The tote can also be used for picnics and other outings. Call Ameda/Egnell (Illinois) at **800/323-8750** for a local distributor or to order direct.

The **HOT + COOL BAG™** (No. 4201, $16 to $17) by Prince Lionheart is a handy, thermally insulated bag that keeps hot things hot and cool things cool for hours. There is room for several jars or bottles, plus an outside front pocket and two tiny side pockets. Worn as a shoulder or waist bag, this bag can be used for storing expressed breast milk, for taking on family outings or going to school or work as a lunch bag. Try using the bag with the optional **HOT + COLD PAK™** (No. 4220, about $16), which is a patented non-toxic gel that can be refrigerated, frozen, boiled or microwaved to provide hours of either cold or heat. For availability see Prince Lionheart on page 68.

If you go the beach or the park sandbox frequently, *be on the lookout for* the **Sandbox Sandbag,** (No. 1002, about $18), a patented, nylon bag for sand toys with drawstring closure that has a special, zippered mesh lining to capture the sand and let you easily empty it. The bag will come in three colors: purple, fuchsia and turquoise. Call Sandbox Industries (New Jersey) at **800/451-6636** for catalogs or local stores.

CAR SEATS AND CAR TRAVEL

When I was shopping for a car seat, my friend Carol told me to call **SafetyBeltSafe U.S.A.** (California). It was truly the best piece of advice for this critically important purchase.

I called their "Safe Ride Helpline" number (**800/745-SAFE**, which has an answering machine, or **310/673-2666**) several times and each time discovered vital information quickly and easily, which would have been virtually impossible to access on my own. SafetyBeltSafe U.S.A. is the only national organization focusing on child passenger safety as its main objective. It offers a toll-free helpline, educational workshops, speakers bureau, an audio-visual library and an outstanding bi-monthly newsletter. Besides knowing the latest car seat recalls, the organization is working hard on such issues as safety belts on school buses (which unbelievably is *not* a law yet), increased safety for children on airplanes and the importance of shoulder belt use in all vehicles.

My first call to SafetyBeltSafe concerned purchasing the safest type of **convertible car seat** (for babies and toddlers who are up to four years of age *and* weigh up to 40 pounds). Their first response was get the one you are most likely to use correctly each and every time that fits your car and is easy to install. The second response was that the "five-point harness" is technically the safest, again provided you use it correctly. It takes a little more work than one with a "T-shield" or one with a larger "tray-shield." (If you do select a T-shield or tray-shield convertible car seat, remember you can't use it with your infant for the first three to six months—you *must* use an infant car seat during this period of time before transferring to a convertible car seat.)

I chose a five-point harness car seat for safety and also because it looked more comfortable than the ones with the T-shield or safety shield, especially since I was going to use the seat with Charlie while he was a tiny infant. (And at the recommendation of SafetyBeltSafe, we used this convertible car seat in a *rear-facing position* until Charlie was age one.)

As I was talking to SafetyBeltSafe, I also mentioned I was already using an **infant car seat** (for babies up to 17 to 20 pounds). When I indicated the brand name and model, I was told that some of the models had a recall—two of the screws needed to be replaced. I was given the recall manufacturing dates and was told where to look on my car seat to find the date. Sure enough, my car seat was under the recall. I then simply called the manufacturer who promptly sent me the correct screws.

Incidentally, an infant car seat is very convenient if you get a model where the seat is detachable from the base (which remains in the car) and can be used as an infant carrier. Whenever you select an infant car seat or a convertible one for that matter, ideally look for one where the safety belt threads through the *base* and not the car seat itself so that you don't have to buckle and unbuckle the safety belt every time (or struggle with a belt that's in the way). Check out this feature for both rear-facing and forward-facing positions. You may have to give up this feature, however, if you can't get a snug fit in one or both positions. Also look for an infant car seat with a hood to keep the sun off your baby.

The next time I called SafetyBeltSafe was when I was in the middle of another recall, this one more major, in which the entire base of my convertible car seat needed to be replaced. I had no luck requesting the base repeatedly from the manufacturer for several months. I called SafetyBeltSafe and found out the name and number of the federal government department and the individual I should contact. The result was that a federal lawyer called the company directly, and I finally received the base. I doubt if I ever would have received the replacement part had it not been for SafetyBeltSafe and the right contact information I received.

If you, too, decide to call SafetyBeltSafe, I recommend you also join the organization by sending in a tax-deductible donation (PO Box 553, Altadena, CA 91003). Chances are you'll be using their helpline repeatedly, and it's a great investment in your child's safety. You can join for as little as $10 a year. With a $25 donation or more, you'll get their "Automatic Updating Service" materials. What I especially like about SafetyBeltSafe is being able to talk with a real person instead of just getting recorded information. They're helpful, too, if you have a baby or child with special needs. I also never realized just how many recalls occur with this type of product and also the many important safety issues that we as parents can help promote.

If all you need is recorded information on recalls, call the **National Highway Traffic Safety Administration (NHTSA)** in Washington, DC, at **800/424-9393** which will send you their latest "Child Safety Seat Recall" package. (See page 141.)

So which car seat should you get? Because there are so many recalls all the time and you need the latest information, I'm not going to recommend a specific brand. Instead here are my suggestions. Reread the information I've presented. Decide which style or styles you'll feel most comfortable with. Call SafetyBeltSafe and ask them to give you three names and models of car seats in the style you prefer—for example, three names of five-point harness car seats that aren't under recall or haven't been in the last several years. Call a store, bring your baby (if possible) and try them out in person as well as in your car. Just as you try on clothes to see if they fit, be sure to check the fit of your car seat before you buy, ideally in your car parked right in the store parking lot. At the very least, make sure your car seat is returnable if you don't have the chance to check the fit. It should be snug like a rock with no slipping for both rear- and front-facing positions. According to Stephanie Tombrello, Executive Director of SafetyBeltSafe, fit should be your first priority. "Your car seat should fit your child, your vehicle and your family's lifestyle."

Finally, balance the benefit of having an infant car seat that doubles as a carrier but will be used only the first year compared with a longer-use convertible car seat. I personally recommend using an infant car seat because it's so convenient and convenience means everything during the first year especially.

.If you buy a T-shield car seat and you live in a place that has either very hot or cold temperatures during the year, Judi's Originals' **Cozi Critters™** (about $18) offer the protection of quilted terry in adorable animal friend covers with ears that

crinkle to a baby's playful touch. My favorites are the elephant (No. 1970001) and the bunny (No. 1970003). Call Judi's Originals at **800/421-9433** for a dealer near you. (No matter what kind of car seat you have, during very hot weather it's a good idea to throw a light-colored towel or blanket over the metal parts or the entire seat to prevent overheating that could burn a baby's skin.)

Finding a cover that universally fits every car seat can be difficult. **Rosie's Babies Deluxe Reversible Fabric/Terry Cloth Fits-All Seat Cover** (No. 2912, about $18) by Diplomat was the answer for us on a difficult-to-fit car seat. The Velcro® brand closures make it easy to adjust this machine washer/dryer safe cover. Cool in summer and warm in winter, the cover comes in a wide range of colors and patterns. Diplomat also has styles for infant car seats and carriers. Call Diplomat Juvenile Corp. in New York at **800/247-9063** for a store near you.

When Charlie takes a snooze, as he often does on extended car trips, it's sure nice to pull out the **Baby Tri-pillow** (No. BTP400, about $13) to support his sleepy, drooping head. It's also useful in the stroller or for sleeping adults on planes, trains or buses. The removable cover is washable and comes in four pastel colors. Call Lamby Nursery Collection (Washington) at **800/669-0527** for a store near you.

When Charlie was 20 pounds and 12 months I turned his car seat to forward-facing in the back seat. It was  difficult to resist the dangerous temptation to turn around and see how he was doing until I discovered **The First Years Car Child View Mirror** (No. 3328, about $5). Then I no longer had to turn around because this handy mirror let me quickly and clearly see Charlie while I'm looking forward. It attaches easily to your rear view mirror, hanging just below, and it adjusts easily, too. For store locations, call The First Years/Kiddie Products, Inc. (Massachusetts) at **800/533-6708**.

If you drive a van then you know that rear visibility is limited. The **Safety 1st Parent's Helper Rearview Magnifier** (No. 206, about $10) increases your rear field of vision. Made for Safety 1st by 3M, it's also good for mini-vans, station wagons and campers.

Also by Safety 1st, the Car-Go Bag (No. 158, about $7) is a handy back seat organizer we use to store Charlie's travel necessities, books and toys. It measures 14 by 18 inches.

TRAVELING MEALS

There are some wonderful items for on-the-go meals that I recommend.

Charlie enjoys the **Safety 1st Lil' Muncher Snack Box** (No.  282, about $2.50). With the two handles, it's easy for little hands to hold. A dry snack holder, the box holds a good supply of crackers. The special lid is easy for an adult to open but not easy for a toddler—which I see as a plus. For store locations call Safety 1st (Massachusetts) at **800/962-7233**.

I also like **The First Years® TumbleMates™ 4 Pack-A-Snack Cups** (No. 1672,  about $4.60), which are four brightly colored 4.5-ounce cups that have four snack dispenser lids with swivel tops. Either you or your toddler can swing the lids open to serve small finger foods, such as crackers or cereal. The swivel tops easily close for travel or storage.

If you're going to grind your own food for your older baby, *be on the lookout for* **The First Years® Compact Food Grinder** (No. 1029, about $10.80) which is a new product I've seen in their catalog that is dishwasher safe. For store locations, call The First Years/Kiddie Products, Inc. (Massachusetts) at **800/533-6708**.

If you're going on a longer trip or even a quick day outing, you may prefer to take Marshall's patented **Happy Baby® Deluxe Food Grinder With Tote**, which is described on page 36 of Chapter 4.

 I like taking the **Fisher-Price® Infant Dish**, (No. 1527, about $7), for traveling because utensils store conveniently in the dish base and the snap-on cover keeps food fresh and safer from spills (although you don't want to have food that is liquified). This microwave-safe dish also has an additional compartment for dry snacks or cereal.

I like three travel items for drinking. If you're going to be traveling with a baby who bottle feeds and you don't want to take bottles that take up a lot of luggage space, bring along **POPUPS™ Expandable Nursers** (No. 8001, $2.50 to $2.70) by

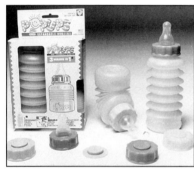 Prince Lionheart. POPUPS hold eight ounces in their fully expanded position (each bellow holds about one ounce of liquid). Collapse POPUPS into their four-ounce size for juice, light feedings or for compact traveling storage. The bellows are also a handy gripping surface for tiny hands. In addition, you can bend this nurser to help trap air and keep it from entering a baby's tummy. Call Prince Lionheart at **800/544-1132** (805/922-2250 in California) for a local store or to order direct.

 For the baby who is learning to use a cup, the **änsa® Sipper** by SmileTote is a cross between the wonderful änsa® Easy-To-Hold® Bottle with the hole in the middle (see page 27 in Chapter 3) and the inno-vative SmileTote self-closing, leak resistent top. Charlie enjoys using the änsa Sipper (about $5.25), which is shown to the left in

open and closed positions. He also enjoys the award-winning **Toddler Traveling Juice Cup** (about $4.25, also shown here) by SmileTote, which also makes a larger **Toddler Tumbler** (about $5.25) that holds nine ounces. These three U.S.-made, SmileTote products are available at Toys R Us, Target, Osco, Wal-Mart and K-Mart.

When we take Charlie out to a restaurant, we like to bring along the **Evenflo® Snack & Play® The Neat Little Eat Seat™** (No. 290101, about $30), which turns most any chair into a high

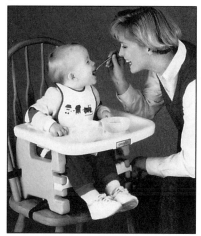

chair. It features both a three-position tray and seat that easily adjust to accommodate a growing toddler. I feel much more comfortable using the Snack & Play than a restaurant-supplied high chair that isn't as clean. It's portable and lightweight and breaks down for travel or storage. I like the carry handle and the color-coded straps for the child and chair. Designed for children six months to 3½ years, this versatile product can also be used for reading, coloring and playing. Without the tray, it becomes a convenient booster seat. Call Evenflo (Ohio) at **800/233-5921** for local stores.

If you know you're going to many places with ample table top space, get the **Graco® Sport Tot-Loc® chair** (No. 3045-29, about $42) which is a high back, no-slip, hook-on chair with a removable tray and patented locking system. It sets up quickly and will fit tables 5/8 inches to 2½ inches thick. Call Graco (Pennsylvania) at **800/345-4109** for store locations.

CHANGING TIME ON THE ROAD

If you're going to be doing a lot of car travel or driving places for extended stays, I recommend a wonderful portable changing table by Baby Bjorn called **Easy Change** (about $110). It's a durable, quality product I've tested, which you can set on the floor or on a table. It's made of a unique, smooth heat reflecting vinyl that warms to the touch in about six seconds and is easy to wipe clean. It has three five-inch-high sides and the changing surface measures 25½ inches long by 12 inches wide. It's designed to position baby so that you can see what you're doing (see also page 8 in Chapter 1). If you have a two-story house, the Easy Change would make a great second changing table downstairs. Call Baby Bjorn (Georgia) at **800/593-5522** for a local store.

Charlie is not quite ready for the next products, but hopefully, he can test them out soon. I plan to get the Safety 1st pocket-size package of 12 self-dispensing **Toilet Seat Covers** (No. 129, about $2) and have Charlie use them with the **Children On the Go Folding Potty Seat** (No. 800, about $10). This seat is larger

than most portable potty seats and is made of a heavier molded plastic, has overhangs in the front to prevent it from sliding back, has overlaps over the hinges to prevent pinching and has four large plastic pads on the bottom to prevent sliding. You can find this seat at Toys R Us, The Right Start Catalog (California) at **800/548-8531**, One Step Ahead (Illinois) at **800/274-8440** or direct from Children On the Go (Illinois) at **800/537-2684**.

We're also waiting for Charlie to test out the award-winning **INFLATE-A-POTTY** (about $15), which inflates in seconds, is

used with eight-gallon trash bags and when deflated fits in a pocket-size carrying pouch that's included. Also included are three disposable bags and ties, disposable tissues and an extension tube for inflating. Order this innovative product that was designed by parents through The Right Start Catalog (California) at **800/548-8531** or the Hand in Hand catalog (Maine) at **800/872-9745** or call Brite-Times (California) at **800/933-6340** for recorded dealer information.

OUT IN PUBLIC HELPERS

There are several protective devices that help you better control an active toddler when in a place where vibrant behavior is either not appropriate or perhaps downright dangerous.

The supermarket is one such place. According to a report by the Consumer Product Safety Commission, "falls from shopping carts are one of the leading causes of serious head injuries to infants and toddlers." So when I put Charlie in a shopping cart, I use a restraining device such as **CARTA-KID** (about $20) by Rock-A-Bye Baby.

Two products in one, the soft, padded, U.S.-made, machine washable CARTA-KID turns your shopping cart into a stroller.

Developed by a mother in association with her pediatrician, this patented safety seat has a cover that prevents teething on most of the handle. You can use the safety cradle from birth to approximately five months and then change to an upright safety seat from five months to three years. (We've used the upright seat position.) Thousands of parents have used CARTA-KID since 1985. I would add an extra soft blanket for additional cushioning for a baby in the safety cradle. The Velcro® straps and easy-to-follow instruction sheet help make this product easy to use. It folds down easily into a small compact bundle for travel. Call Rock-A-Bye Baby (Florida) at **800-ROCK-A-BYE (800/762-5229)** for the nearest retailer or The Baby Club of America (Connecticut) at **800/PLAYPEN (800/752-9736)** to order by phone.

A couple of body harnesses can double as shopping cart restraining devices. Tot Tenders makes a darling one Charlie wears called **Tot Tether** (about $30), which comes in six friendly

animal styles, all with a "tail" tether that attaches to the parent. A built-in backpack is handy for snacks, small toys and books. Beautifully crafted and sewn, this U.S.-made harness/backpack is fun to use, adjusts for new walkers through preschoolers and can be hand washed. Call Tot Tenders (Oregon) at **800/634-6870** for local dealers or to order direct.

Be on the lookout for **Ride 'N Stride** ($12 to $13), a Velcro® closure toddler body harness by Leachco that has different color-coded straps and doubles as a shopping cart restraint. This one will be cooler in summer than the Tot Tether which has more material. You can order from One Step Ahead (Illinois) at **800/274-8440** or call Leachco (Oklahoma) at **800/525-1050** for local stores.

OTHER OVERNIGHT HELPERS

Here are two more items to have on hand if you're going to be doing a lot of traveling from early on.

The **Travel Tub™** (No.

129, about $15) by Cosco is a molded baby bath that folds (as shown) for travel and storage. It fits most kitchen sinks including double sinks and stores baby's bath supplies for traveling. The lift-up lid locks in place to form a back support and a removable cushioned insert is designed to comfortably position your baby. It also has a built-in soap dish. The tub can be used as a travel case. Call Cosco (Indiana) at **800/544-1108** for local store names.

The **Fisher-Price® 3-in-1 Travel Tender With Bassinet** (No. 9156, about $120) is a portable bassinet, crib and playpen. It has an easy, pop-open assembly and comes with a vinyl mattress pad, fitted sheet and storage bag. I examined this versatile product at the JPMA show. It weighs about 21 pounds. Check availability of the Travel Tender at major retailers such as Toys R Us, Wal-Mart, K-Mart and Target or call Fisher-Price (New York) **800/432-KIDS** for stores near you.

8

The Best
Dressed Baby

We've been fortunate to have friends and relatives give Charlie many high quality new clothes as well as hand-me-downs. Since I'm very practical when it comes to clothing, this chapter has items with special functional features. You'll find little in the way of layette items (you'll do better to check the books listed in Chapter 12 on pages 134-37). But I'm sure you'll discover some exciting items that make dressing a whole lot easier.

FOOTWEAR

Starting from the feet up, here are some of my favorites. There are all kinds of baby socks and booties, but I really liked **The First Years Comfy-Cuff Booties** (No. 3701, about $2.10). These kept Charlie's feet warm and they stayed on! The cuff is elasticized at the ankle for a snug, comfortable fit for active little feet. They come in two sizes, zero to six months (No. 3701) and six to 12 months (No. 3702). For store locations, call The First Years/Kiddie Products (Massachusetts) at **800/533-6708**.

Experts agree that first shoes for babies should be soft, breathable, flexible, squared off at the toes and resemble the natural barefoot state. Charlie has enjoyed **Padders®** soft bootie/shoes ($7 to $10). They're great as a training shoe when your baby is learning to walk. Padders protect feet and keep

them warm but allow them to grow and develop naturally. They're also great as slippers. Made of corduroy, cotton or denim, Padders are completely machine washable and easy to put on. They stay on with an elastic closure at the ankles. Call Padders Inc. (New York) at **800/ 7PADDERS (800/772-3337)** for local stores.

Charlie's first walking shoe was the **Stride Rite® First Move**

(about $34), which is the first and only baby shoe to carry the APMA Seal of Acceptance for the American Podiatric Medical Association. A U.S.-made leather shoe, it is machine-washable and comes in all white or white with pink. Stride Rite designed this shoe for the "Early Walking Stage" of its "Progression System," which identifies three stages of walking ability.

Charlie's next shoe (and the one he's now wearing) is Stride Rite's **Baby Tech™** (about $39) in soil-resistent, fun colors—green,

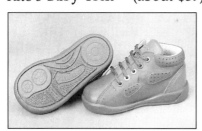

blue and red. (It's also available in a fuchsia and lilac combination or all white.) This shoe has a soft, breathable leather "upper" that offers freedom of movement, durability and easy care. The dual-density Dynatech™ soles with shock absorbing inserts provide for added cushioning and comfort. Direct injection construction attaches the upper to the sole without cements or stitching, resulting in maximum flexibility and optimum performance for early to intermediate walkers. Call Stride Rite (Massachusetts) at **800/662-9788** for your nearest dealer.

And here's another name you can trust in children's shoes: Buster Brown, a shoe company and brand name that dates back to 1904. Two baby Buster Brown shoes worthy of attention are

Itty Bitty Busters™ ($15 to $20), which are pre-walk shoes for infants, and **My First Buster™** ($25 to $35), a toddler's first walking shoe (two styles are shown here). My First Buster recently received the Good Housekeeping Seal of Approval. My First Buster incorporates technical advances aimed toward helping young feet develop properly. "Buster-Flex Grooves" in the sole let the shoe flex and bend where a child's foot naturally flexes and bends. The "Springboard Innersole" combines stability in the heel and toe areas along with unrestricted flexibility across the ball of the foot. The "Padded Sock Lining, Collar & Tongue" provide comfort and protection. Quality leather uppers are hand washable, lightweight and breathable. This shoe comes in five different styles. Call **800/225-4371, ext. 100** (Missouri) for names of local department stores and independent children's shoe stores that carry Buster Brown.

BEAUTIFUL BASICS
Start your newborn off right in Gerber's **Onesies® One-Piece Underwear,** ($9 to $10 for a three-pack) versatile underwear invented by Gerber that provides the convenience of an undershirt and a diaper cover in one piece, making diaper changing easy with a snap crotch. There are no side seams and the non-chafing arm construction protects a baby's tender skin. It comes in five sizes: Newborn (up to 12 pounds), Small (13 to 18 pounds), Medium (19 to 26 pounds), Large (27 to 34 pounds) and Extra Large (35 to 42 pounds).

And now Gerber has introduced **Funsie Onesies™** ($5 to $6)

that feature novelty character screen print designs (such as the one shown here) in bright fashion colors. Small, Medium and Large sizes are available. Much more than underwear, Funsie Onesies are cute enough to be worn as a body shirt with pants, shorts, leggings or a skirt. I have used and enjoyed both versatile Onesie products with Charlie. Onesies are available at mass merchandisers and you can call **Gerber (Michigan) at 800/4-GERBER (800/443-7237)** to find local stores that sell their products.

My favorite playwear is made by **OshKosh B'Gosh**. I especially love their classic **Bib Overall** (about $22) with the hickory stripe that Aunt Barbara and Uncle Burt gave him. I like that OshKosh B'Gosh clothing is sized larger than other manu-facturers' garments, and with the adjustable straps and cuffs that roll up on the Bib Overall, Charlie has gotten a lot of extra mileage out of this piece alone.

For nearly a century, OshKosh B'Gosh has been a household word in the U.S. Beginning operations in Oshkosh, Wisconsin, in 1895, with bib overalls for frontier railroad workers and

farmers, the company began making overalls for children in the early 1900s so that kids could dress like their fathers. Today children's sizes range from newborn through size 14 and include layette, dresses, activewear, swimwear, sleepwear, outerwear, sweats, shoes and accessories. OshKosh is known for its expert workmanship, durability and styling and has won numerous design awards. Most of the clothes are made in one of the 17 U.S. manufacturing facilities. Capable of mixing and matching with one another, each OshKosh B'Gosh garment can also stand alone.

The "Classics" line is available year round and includes popular traditional styles such as the **Traditional Bib Overall** ($19.50 to $27.50) and **Traditional Shortall** ($17.50 to $24.50) for baby/toddler boys and the softer, fuller **Busy Body Bib Overalls** ($19.50 to $25.50), **Busy Body Shortalls** ($18.50 to $23) and **Busy**

Body Jumpers ($17 to $25.50) for baby/toddler girls. Don't overlook the wonderful classic OshKosh B'Gosh tops, most of which have two buttons at the neck for easier dressing.

But the Classics line is just the tip of the iceberg. You'll also see special "seasonal" collections with exciting new prints, colors, fabrics and designs. And with separates that work with both the collections and the Classics line, you have a tremendous number of quality pieces that will mix and match. (The photos show examples of a toddler boy's bib overall and a toddler girl's shortall from two different collections.)

Multiple-award winning OshKosh B'Gosh clothing is available nationally through fine department and specialty stores and catalogs. For store locations, call one of these four regional offices: Eastern (New York), **212/947-5022;** Western (California), **213/623-6243;** Northern (Illinois), **312/645-0847;** and Southern (Texas), **214/631-8831.**

Healthtex is a name you can trust for quality everyday playwear. The **Healthtex Bodyshirt™** ($11 to $13) shown here can be worn by itself or with a bottom. It features a snap shoulder with an extra-wide neck opening, a durable snap crotch and finished legs. It solves the problem of keeping your infant's shirt tucked in and tummy covered. The Bodyshirt is available in 12-, 18- and 24-month sizes.

Healthtex Playwear Denims™ for infants and toddlers offer the best of denim (comfortable yet durable 100 percent cotton, 10-ounce fabric) in garments designed without constricting seams so that they go in every direction your infant or toddler goes. Fabric-covered elastic waists and leg openings and double-knees in the pants provide added comfort and durability. Playwear Denims are available in overalls, pants, shorts, jumpers and skirts and come in 12-, 18- and 24-month sizes as well as 2T through 6x/7.

With the exception of Playwear Denims, all Healthtex garments are made with a soft cotton/polyester blend that's easy to wash and requires little or no ironing. Healthtex offers both soft, traditional pastel colors and bright, primary colors. With nice, wide neck openings, extra snaps and outfits that are slightly larger for a comfortable fit, there's an emphasis on easy dressing for both parent and baby.

Consumer oriented, Healthtex offers a one-year garment warranty that's listed on the "hangtag." The warranty is printed in English and Spanish. There's also a helpful height/weight sizing chart. Also on the tag is an 800 number, **800/554-7637** (North Carolina), which can direct you to a store that carries Healthtex.

For soft, durable, brightly colored playwear that features a three-inch "growable cuff" to assure a perfect fit with room to grow, check out Gymboree Stores. At this writing there are 112 stores in 23 states; there should be over 145 stores by the end of 1993. The stores themselves are pleasant places to shop with "stroller-friendly" gym floors and interactive Gymboree music videos to entertain children while parents shop. The stores and clothing reflect the fun quality of the Gymboree Play Program, which is described on page 142 of Chapter 12.

ON-THE-GO ACCESSORIES

One accessory I would want next time for my newborn is **The First Years No Scratch Baby Mitts** (No. 3700, two pairs about $3.50). Designed to fit over tiny infant hands to protect babies from scratching themselves, the mitts could also be used to protect babies' hands from strangers who can't resist touching those dainty little fingers. Also for indoor use, the mitts can be reversed to cover just the fingers, freeing a baby's thumb for sucking.

The next two products are especially important if you live in sunny, bright places (although ultraviolet protection is actually important for baby's tender eyes and skin no matter where you

live). Absolutely indispensable is **Flap Happy® The Original Flap Hat** (about $10) with its broad brim and generous flap that protect a baby's face and neck from the sun. Charlie has worn these hats ever since he was a young baby. The hat is available in department stores, boutiques and catalogs; call Flap Happy, Inc. (California) at **800/234-FLAP (800/234-3527)** for names.

To some, baby sunglasses may seem like a frivolous fashion

item. But in view of the fact that babies' retinas are more susceptible to the sun's ultraviolet (UV) damage, experts recommend special protection, especially when exposed to direct or reflected sunlight. **Baby Optics Sunglasses** (about $15) were created five years ago to provide ophthalmic quality sunglasses for babies and toddlers. Made with polycarbonate impact resistant lenses (the safest, lightest and highest quality lens material), these sunglasses give UV-400 protection (the maximum), have rounded edged frames, are lightweight and use non-toxic materials. Charlie has worn these protective yet adorable glasses from early on. They come in four sizes: Newborn, zero to six months; Baby, six months to two years; Tots, two to four years; and Kids, five to nine years. Call Baby Optics (Utah) at **800/962-6874** for a local store.

Another essential on-the-go accessory, especially in the summer when Charlie's wearing shorts, is Marran International's patented, U.S.-made **Baby Bumpers®** knee pads (about $7). Every time we go on an outing and Charlie's wearing his Baby Bumpers, several people always come up to me and remark what a great idea they

are. They prevent cuts, bruises and scrapes to babies' and toddlers' knees. I usually put them on Charlie when he's still buckled in his car seat or stroller. They're great for crawlers or walkers (from six to 30 months). You can also put them on *over* clothing to prevent wear and tear. Three quarter-inch thick, the pads are made of plush, high grade foam, are shaped to fit around knees and are adjustable with Velcro® straps. They are machine washer/dryer safe. You can find Baby Bumpers in most baby stores nationwide, The Right Start Catalog (California) at **800/548-8531** or call Marran International (California) at **310/271-9911** for a local store.

OTHER ACCESSORIES
Here are three handy accessories that solve special clothing problems.

For the tops that never seem to stay tucked in, **Shirt Anchors** (about $5) from American Baby Concepts may be the answer. I've used these anchors on some of Charlie's shorter shirts. The trick is to put the anchors on the shirt first before putting the shirt on your baby.

To extend the life of creepers, rompers, or body shirts that have a snap crotch, U.S.-made **False Bottoms** garment extender (No. 1280 has two snaps, No. 1281 has three snaps, about $5.50 for two pairs) also by American Baby Concepts, snaps into the crotch of a baby's garment to make it larger and can extend the useful life of baby's clothing for months. Call **800/537-7181** (Iowa) for store or catalog names for these two items.

For the pajama sleepers with legs and feet that are too big

BEFORE   AFTER

and for long pant cuffs that just don't stay rolled up, **Uncle Randy's Baby Garters** ($4 to $5) by American Baby Products are the answer to help prevent tripping. ("Before" and "after" pictures show the difference these garters can make.) Almost one million of these U.S.-made garters have sold. Charlie has tested these out and he approves. They're available through the **Perfectly Safe Catalog** (Ohio) at **800/837-KIDS**.

9

The Best Toys
for Babies

What difficult choices parents and children's gift givers face with more than 150,000 toys in the market and 2,000 new ones each year (plus all the books, tapes and videos)! Try going into any toy store (let alone a mass merchandiser) without having some idea of what you want to buy. You'll probably quickly go into a state of overwhelm.

While I certainly haven't seen or tested all of the toy, tape and book merchandise in the world, I feel blessed to have discovered some real winners. Most have been tested by me and/or Charlie. Many have won awards. Some I haven't reviewed personally but have received special reviews or recognition or are made by companies I trust. It's my hope that the following will provide some helpful suggestions for you from the current merchandise maze but *no baby should have all of the products included in this and the next two chapters.*

Before we look at this chapter's toys for "babies" (from birth to one year), let me share a few criteria I apply as both a parent and an educator when selecting toys.

I want safe, durable toys that are age appropriate. By the way, the age ranges that manufacturers give, including the ones listed here, refer more to *safety* guidelines, not necessarily age appropriate, developmental guidelines. For the latter, it's essential to get to know your baby or toddler to understand their interests and abilities.

The Consumer Product Safety Commission (CPSC) has put together a wonderful listing of interests, abilities and suggested toys by different age groups, starting with infants called "**Which Toy For Which Child: A Consumer's Guide to Selecting Suitable Toys, Ages Birth Through Five.**" (See page 141 for information on how to get this CPSC listing as well as other CPSC publications.) This listing is also reprinted in the book *The Perfectly Safe® Home* (see page 51). This listing is my bible whenever I go toy shopping. Also helpful is the four-page *Parent and preschooler* newsletter, Volume 5, No. 9, by Dr. Michael Meyerhoff (Massachusetts) at **617/237-3333**.

I like toys that are versatile and interesting (ideally to both me and Charlie, but mostly for him). Meyerhoff calls this versatility "play value." I like what he says about cost versus play value: "The *cost* of a toy usually increases with the number of things that it does, whereas the *play value* of a toy increases with the number of things that a child can do with it." I look for toys that offer many different possibilities for Charlie, appeal to a variety of senses or learning experiences and include a range of different skills and abilities he will develop over time.

CRIB TOYS

In Chapter 1 I talked about using a mobile over the changing area. Undoubtedly, you'll want one for the crib. I prefer a softer, more soothing pastel-colored mobile in a crib, especially for a new baby, when your goal is to provide a restful, comforting environment. (For more active, alert times you might use a "high-contrast" mobile in the crib or over the changing area—see pages 14-15 for a more detailed discussion on high contrast versus pastels.) I'd also get one that's battery-operated rather than a wind-up mechanism.

The best crib mobile I've seen and tested is the versatile and extended-use **CribEssentials™ Mobile and Musical Crib Light** (about $35) by Pansy Ellen Products because it's three easy-to-use products in one: a mobile with an on-off switch and adorable pastel bears and blocks or balloons that face your baby, a music box that plays Brahms Lullaby and a push button crib light. And when your baby outgrows the mobile, you can remove the figures and holder from the crib but leave the combination crib light/music box on the rail or set it on a dresser. Three settings let you decide to use the mobile with: 1) music, movement and crib light 2) just music and movement or 3) crib light only. On

top of that, all settings can be manually activated by pushing a button or voice activated (your baby's voice or cry, not yours). The music will play for five minutes at a stretch and automatically turn off after that. The mobile fits standard cribs but Pansy Ellen will send you a free adapter for your Euro-style crib if you call to request it. Besides soothing and comforting, this mobile entertains your baby while also developing important auditory and visual tracking skills. It operates on four "C" batteries that aren't included. The mobile is available in retail chains nationwide and you can call Pansy Ellen (Georgia) at **404/751-0442** for a local one.

Infants up to two months like to see and hear interesting things and enjoy variety. (Toys for watching should be about 8 to 14 inches from their eyes at first.) I really like a couple of Century's crib toys because they are visually interesting, make sounds and detach for close-up play. **Century® Cribanimals™**

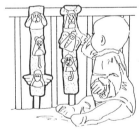

(No. 170-302, $14 to $16) can attach to a crib as well as a stroller, carrier or car seat. There are two sets of three animals each, one set in primary colors and the other in pastel for variety and to reflect the different moods of your baby. The darling animal pals (which are washable) squeak, crinkle and rattle and detach from fabric sleeves.

The **Crib Rail Barnyard™** (No. 170-308, about $20), shown at the top of the next page, includes a squeaker lamb, teether duck, rattle horse and crinkle cow. Velcro® tabs make this barnyard easy to attach to a crib. Older babies will like this interactive toy, too; the vinyl pocket for the teether and swing-open door will help build eye-hand coordination. Call Century (Ohio) at **800/837-4044** for local store names.

If one barnyard is good, two are better especially if it's made by Little Tikes. Machine washer and dryer safe, the **Barnyard Crib Center** (No. 1533, $16 to $19), shown in the middle of this

page just below, is a soft quilted barn that attaches easily to the crib. I like the different textures and sounds of the crinkling fluffy sheep, the rattling soft cow and the squeaking terry cloth pig. The animals attach with hook and loop fasteners and fit in pockets or can be removed for separate play. The hayloft flap squeaks and when lifted, reveals a cute barn scene. Little Tikes products are at all major retail chain stores, toy discounters and small toy stores as well as the J.C. Penney catalog. You can also call Little Tikes (Ohio) at **800/321-0183** for local retailers.

Large unbreakable mirrors are wonderful for the crib (and other areas, too) but keep in mind that the peak interest in mirrors is between four to six months—you don't have to rush out and buy one for your newborn baby's crib. I have three favorites that would be on my wish list "next time."

The **Fisher-Price® Big View Mirror** (No. 1132, about $12) has a unique curve design that lets babies see more of their world, especially important when they're not yet sitting up. I also like the rounded shape of this mirror and the colorful roller drum with rattling beads and bold graphics. This mirror just won a Parents' Choice Expert Recommendation. Major retailers such as Toys R Us, Wal-Mart, K-Mart and Target should carry this product or call Fisher-Price (New York) at **800/432-KIDS (800/432-5437)** for other stores near you.

Once your baby is sitting up, a nice big mirror such as the **Wimmer-Ferguson Double-Feature Mirror** (described on pages 14-15 of Chapter 1) or the **Pansy Ellen Bright Starts™ Crib Mirror** (about $20) is an excellent choice. The Bright Starts mirror,

which is shown here, measures about 11 by 9 inches (with the frame it's about 13 by 13 inches). What makes this mirror special is the combination of visual and auditory stimulation and entertainment it offers. There is a music box that plays three melodies plus a light show of a glowing moon and twinkling stars. The music will play for 45 seconds and will automatically shut off. It will resume at the sound of your baby's voice or cry. (You can also turn off the music and/or lights.) When your baby outgrows the crib, the mirror can be hung on the wall. It operates on four "AA" batteries that aren't included. The mirror is available in retail chains nationwide and you can call Pansy Ellen (Georgia) at **404/751-0442** for a local one.

FIRST TOYS
When my husband and I were new parents with very little toy experience with babies but with plenty of sleep deprivation, we were thrilled to discover the **Child Development Toys Program** from Parents® Magazine. Designed for babies, starting from birth to nine months, this program delivers at least one educational toy every four to six weeks (for about a year), timed to correspond to your baby's development.

These are "educational toys" for both baby and parent; I

learned a tremendous amount about Charlie's development just by reading the wonderful "Play and Learning™ Guide" that came with each toy. Each illustrated guide provides a summary of the infant research that goes into each toy and gives you practical suggestions and ideas about the many ways you and your baby can use the toy to have fun and develop skills at the same time. The toys are designed by infant-behavior experts, child psychologists, pediatricians and design engineers.

Each shipment costs no more than $15 or as little as $10 (plus shipping) and you don't have to buy every shipment. You can't order toys separately but some of them are available through retail stores (although the pricing is better through the Child Development Toy direct mail program).

Some of Charlie's early favorites (pictured on the prior page and this page in order) were the **Tracking Tube,** which has a bright red floating ball that vanishes into one of two yellow caps that are teethable (one also squeaks); **Wiggle Worm,** an easy-to-hold combination cuddle toy and teether that has different textures and sounds; and **Red Rings,** which is great for pulling, reaching, shaking, twisting and of course, teething. To sign up for the program call Gruner + Jahr USA Publishing at **212/878-8700,** write them at 685 Third Avenue, New York, NY 10017 or fax them at **212/986-4449.**

I remember shopping for a "play or activity gym," a standing A-frame with suspended toys. I stood in the store, looking at all the gyms, not really knowing which one to buy. I finally ending up with one that had thin poles for legs and later proved to be unstable as Charlie became more mobile. There are two I'd buy today because they're more stable and also because they have detachable toys.

The **Fisher-Price® Activity Links Gym** (No. 1090, about $25) is a sturdy play gym with detachable links. There are six fun

activities and sounds, including a shiny mirror, rattling puppy and kitty, colorful spinner and a rattle roller drum. Major retailers such as Toys R Us, Wal-Mart, K-Mart and Target should carry this product or call Fisher-Price (New York) at **800/432-KIDS (800/432-5437)** for other stores near you.

I'm really excited, however, about **Today's Kids GymFinity™** (No. 330, about $34), which is the first infant-to-toddler activity gym, and is a multiple award winner (including a 1992 Parents'

Choice Gold Award and a 1991 Oppenheim Toy Portfolio

selection). Charlie and I have tested out this gym and we approve. It has suspended black and white, three-dimensional animals and graphics for early visual and tactile stimulation (there are a swinging panda and a puppy that are especially cute and a mirror is also included). Three different positions for the top put toys within easy reach for lying or sitting infants. (Even newborns in an infant seat can reach the suspended toys.) For toddlers, the top becomes a bright, exciting activity center of moving gears, shape sorting, drop-throughs and puzzle pieces.

All the pieces are detachable and can be positioned in new, interesting ways. Because Charlie chews on everything, he's discovered the detachable gears. Durable, though not designed specifically for teething, each gear has a knob that Charlie has learned to puncture with his sharp teeth. We've removed the gears at this time. It's so important to observe your child's play, see how toys are used (or misused) and remove them when necessary. I've also called Today's Kids because ideally I'd like to see completely teethable pieces on Gymfinity.

Notwithstanding, this is the gym I would buy for my next baby. I like the stable, three-sided construction of the legs. While GymFinity can easily be moved by a walking baby, it's stable and isn't likely to topple over. It's easy to assemble, too (with no tools!). Today's Kids toys are available at Toys R Us, K-Mart, Target and Service Merchandise or call Today's Kids (Arkansas) at **800/258-TOYS (800/258-8697)** for local stores.

TEETHERS AND SMALL ACTIVITY TOYS
You can't have enough teethers, rattles and little manipulative toys for babies three or four months and up. You should stash these items in your changing areas (great for diverting restless or resistant babies), play areas, diaper bag, stroller and car. Charlie's favorites have been interesting ones with a variety of shapes, sounds, textures and graphics. They could be used in a variety

of ways and were easy for him to hold or manipulate. (Just make sure that when your baby has barely enough motor coordination to hold such toys, that she/he can do so without flinging them wildly around. When Charlie first was able to grasp small toys, we'd have to watch closely to make sure he didn't accidentally hit himself with them.)

Age designations on such toys can be misleading. Almost all rattles say "From Birth." Obviously, babies themselves won't be holding and playing with rattles by themselves. As with any toy, there are many different levels of use. As you select these or any other toys think about the ways you could use each toy *with* your baby as well as how your baby could use it alone.

Discovery Toys makes a number of very interesting little toys for babies. Charlie loved the **Tons of Fun® Rattle** (No. 1010,

about $7), which is shown here. This easy-to-hold, ear-wiggling, tail-wagging, tummy-spinning elephant has bright colors, moving parts and chewable ears. Next time I'd also get their **Spin, Rattle 'N' Roll™ Activity Rattle** (No. 1250, about $10), which is a miniature activity center with a smiling and rattling sun, a spin-

ning spaceman, a sliding rocketship and an orbiting planet; the **Gummy Yummy** (No. 1090, about $7), which is a scented teether with five different textured ends; and **Tumble Time** (No. 1220, about $10), an easy-handling miniature hour-glass with brightly colored beads and handles. Call Discovery Toys (California) at **800/426-4777** for the name of your local "consultant" who personally shows and sells their toys.

Charlie really enjoyed **The First Years First Keys** (No. 2049, about $1.55), which have smooth, round edges and a large key

ring and are shown here. Great for teething, these colorful keys swing freely and are numbered, so your baby can use them later as a counting toy. Next time I'd also get their **Soft Handled Teether Rattle** (No. 2110, about $5) that combines rolling balls in a double-sealed spinning center with four soft teethable, easy-to-grasp handles.

The First Years makes two other small rattles I have seen and recommend. The **Hide 'N Seek Rattle** (No. 2115, about $4.10) is

shaped like a diaper pin and has bright red and blue balls that

disappear into one end
and then run out again.
The **Chime Rattle** (No.
2129, about $3), has
soothing chime sounds, fun
pictures, a soft protective
cushion for teething safety
and an easy-grasp handle
for holding or teething. For store locations, call The First
Years/Kiddie Products (Massachusetts) at **800/533-6708**.

Gerber makes four little rattles I like. The **Sea Shell™ Rattle**
(No. 76352, $1.80) features visible colored beads inside a clear-
tinted (blue or pink), high-impact plastic, safety-sealed shell
design. The **Happy Elephant™ Mirror Rattle** (No. 76314, about
$1.65), has a good quality, break resistent mirror and durable
plastic construction that houses rattling beads. It comes in dark
pink, blue or yellow. The **Shake 'N Spin Rattle** (No. 76315,
about $2.35), is a durable sonic-sealed plastic frame surrounding
a clear spiral rattle containing colorful beads that tumble down,
helping to develop eye tracking skills while entertaining your
baby. The rounded corners and open design allow for safe, easy
grasping. The **Spinning Teether Rattle™** (No. 76304, about $2.40)
is similar with durable plastic handles and frame and an open
design. A clear ball in the center has colorful beads that a baby
can shake.

Safety 1st makes two teethers I've seen and I recommend for
older babies (or toddlers) who are still teething. The **Baby
Cassette Teether** (No. 146, about $2.50) is a teether and action
toy in one. It has a removable soft teething cassette, a rattle
sound, an on/off clicker and soft teething buttons. Their **Circus
Teethers** (No. 149, about $2) combine bright colors, realistic
animal detailing and hard and soft materials. A handy clip-on
ring attaches to the stroller or crib.

I've seen the new Fisher-Price® **Cow Bells Rattle** (No. 1439,
about $3.60) in their catalog and it looks fun with its easy-to-
grasp black and white cow and the clattering sound of the
movable, primary-colored bells. (For availability, see Fisher-Price
on page 94.)

Charlie really enjoyed the **Playskool® Click 'N Swirl Rattle**
(No. 5122, about $2.60) that family friend Marilyn brought over
one day. It's a fun first phone that features colorful beads and a
click-around dial. *Be on the lookout for* the new **Fun 'n Fruity™**

 **Teether** (No. 3158, about $3.20), which comes in three soft, colorful fruits (watermelon, orange and lemon) and is shown here. This teether offers two ways to relieve teething pain: the special textured areas around the edge of the teether gently massage gums, and the water-filled middle acts as a soothing cold compress. Playskool products such as these are available through mass merchandisers and other stores and you can call Playskool (Rhode Island) at **401/431-TOYS (401/431-8697)** for local store names.

TOYS FROM SIX MONTHS

At about "six months" most babies seem to be able to do a lot more physically. They are beginning to sit up by themselves, to creep, crawl and move about more proficiently, developing "pincer" (thumb-and-finger) grasp and small muscle coordination and having a lot of fun exploring the physical properties of the objects around them. Here are some toys Charlie enjoyed as well as others I would have liked to have had.

Charlie really enjoyed the Little Tikes® **Play About**™ **House**

 (No. 1518, $17 to $19), a stimulating, three-dimensional floor activity center that's loaded with activities on both sides of the fantasy house. It includes Toddle Tots® friends that slide down the chimney, make a bell ring and open the door. It also includes a spinning, clear ball with brightly colored beads, two bright springs for batting, colorful rings that slide back and forth, a clicking phone dial, a squeaking lever, a spring-ing jiggle face and a spinning candy cane handle. Although Little Tikes suggests this for ages 3 months to 3 years, I believe the optimal age range is more like six to 15 months. (For availability see Little Tikes on page 92.)

Our friends Linda, Stan and Lauren gave Charlie the Playskool **Busy Camera** (No. 5079, about $7) when he was almost exactly six months. He loved all the activities on this wonderful toy camera: peek-a-boo door, spinning "lens," pop-up buttons, "shutter" squeaker, and clicking "film advance" knob. It also has a built in carry handle for take-along play. I think he particularly liked this toy because he could mimic me (I was continually taking pictures of him) and because a camera is a wonderful way to play peek-a-boo. The **Busy Guitar** (No. 5131, about $9.25) also looks like a fun choice with five fun activities and sounds. It includes tuning pegs that click, a ratcheting pick, a spinning musical chime, a squeaker button and two push and pop buttons that make a "boing-boing" sound. Playskool suggests both these toys for ages six to 24 months. (For availability see Playskool on page 98.)

Mirrors are great and Discovery Toys' **Rolling Reflections** (No. 1140, about $15) is a mirror on wheels with jingling bells that is designed to stay upright even as the wheels are turning. Stimulating visual and auditory senses, while developing "gross  motor skills" by encouraging a baby to crawl after the rolling mirror, this toy just won a Parents' Choice Expert Recommendation. I examined this quality mirror and approve it, also. (Gross motor skills refer to activities performed by the large muscle groups, such as sitting, crawling, standing, walking, running, jumping and throwing.) The suggested age is listed as "from six months."

Also for gross motor skills, don't overlook the importance of introducing balls that your baby can roll, hold, drop and eventually throw and kick. The Discovery Toys **TANGIBALL** (No. 1340, about $9) makes a wonderful, bright blue, squeezable ball that squeaks, is easy-to-hold with hundreds of knobby nubs, is teethable and has a soft vanilla scent. (For availability see Discovery Toys on page 96.)

Sometimes you get a gift that at first glance looks too old for your baby. The Texas Instruments **Listen & Learn™ Nursery Rhymes Ball** (about $25) was such a gift that turned out to be a real favorite with Charlie. It stimulated his motor development by encouraging him to crawl toward the ball and rewarded him with a nursery song or melody each time he successfully was able to push the ball in a different direction. And what a wonderful way to introduce him to language and music!

The Listen & Learn Nursery Rhymes is a sturdy, bright-blue, 12-sided picture ball that can be turned or rolled. When the ball stops turning, it plays the nursery rhyme depicted by the illustration that is facing up. Six rhymes have vocals; six are

instrumental versions. If left alone for a few seconds, the ball tries to re-attract a baby's attention with a short melody. If no further play occurs, the product says, "Bye-bye," and turns itself off to prolong battery life. (It uses two "AA" batteries.) The sound quality in this toy, unlike many other "talking" toys, is excellent. The suggested age range is six to 36 months. Texas Instruments toys can be found in Toys R Us stores nationwide as well as other toy and discount stores and you can call Texas Instruments (Texas) at **800/TI-CARES (800/842-2737)** for local retailers.

Fisher-Price has three toys I like that they suggest may be introduced at six months. The **Activity Walker** (No. 1040, about $30) is a floor activity center I would get "next time" that converts to a stable walker with fun clicking sounds. It also

converts into a play cart or toy stroller later on. It folds flat for carrying and storage. The suggested ages are six to 36 months. (While called a "walker," this isn't the typical walker, which consists of a seat set inside a four-wheeled framework. I'm not in favor of the typical walker, which has been associated with many accidents. I've also read that a walker doesn't speed up the walking process. Charlie didn't use one and I have deliberately omitted this type of product from *Baby's Best!*)

Charlie is still enjoying two inexpensive Fisher-Price toys, the **Rock-A-Stack®** rings (No. 1050, about $6) and **Baby's First Blocks** (No. 1024, about $9). Five colorful plastic rings in the Rock-A-Stack fit over a cone with a rocking base in sequence of rainbow colors and graduated sizes. This deceptively simple toy teaches many concepts such as colors, size differences and sequencing by size and may take a baby several years to master them all. (The suggested age range is six to 36 months.)

Baby's First Blocks, shown below, were Charlie's  first, too. This toy took many months to master but we introduced it at around six months (which may be too early for many babies). Twelve colorful blocks come in three different shapes (circle, triangle and square) that can be dropped through the canister's shape sorter top or simply played with by themselves. The suggested ages are six to 24 months.

TOYS FROM NINE MONTHS

Two other early shape sorting toys I like give a suggested starting age of nine months. One is the Texas Instruments **Musical Shape & Sort™** (about $25), which was the first electronic sorting product and was introduced in 1992. This sorter has a base with three clear sorting tubes and three shapes, a red circle, a blue square and a green triangle. There are several activities Charlie was able to master. First he learned to drop each shape into its correct tube, listening to the shape's accompanying whistling sound as it went down the tube (provided the piece was dropped right side up). Second, he learned to depress the activity switches that release the shapes and in doing so, he heard one of three tunes for each shape. Third, Charlie made up his own activity by blowing into a shape and recreating the whistling sound on his own. The durable Musical Shape & Sort is good for reinforcing colors and developing hand-eye coordination, motor and auditory memory skills and was selected by the November, 1992, issue of *Parents*

Magazine as one of the best toys of 1992. The suggested age range is nine to 24 months. You can call Texas Instruments (Texas) at **800/TI-CARES (800/842-2737)** for local retailers. (If by any chance you should receive or have a Musical Shape & Sort that was purchased before August 17, 1992, you'll want to contact Texas Instruments Consumer Relations at the same number and ask them for a "retrofit kit.")

The First Years has two inexpensive, yet quality toys I like for age nine months and up, including a traveling shape sorter. I like the **Fit 'N Fill Discovery Pail** (No. 2605, about $8.50) because it's a small pail with a convenient handle. There are six blocks (two for each shape).

Charlie has enjoyed **My First Puzzle** (No. 2608, about $4.50),

which is a simple, four-piece plastic puzzle that features four different colored fruit shapes with easy-to-grasp knobs. The name of the fruit is printed in the same color of the fruit on the puzzle board. The puzzle is also available with animal shapes (No. 2605) as shown in the picture. See also bath toys on pages 47-49 in Chapter 5, sitting and rocking toys on pages 58-62 in Chapter 6 and toddler toys in Chapter 10, the next chapter.

10

The Best Toys
for Toddlers

The toys in this section are for toddlers who are ages one to three years. Since that's a big age range I will indicate more specific ages as necessary. If you haven't read the toy selection criteria presented on pages 89-90 of Chapter 9, please do so before reading this chapter.

I've organized these toys into three categories: gross motor, fine motor and traveling toys. Toys that build "gross motor" skills help with activities performed by the large muscle groups, such as walking, climbing, running, jumping, kicking and throwing. Toys that build "fine motor" skills help develop hand-eye coordination and use of the hands and fingers to manipulate and arrange objects. (Of course, there will be some overlap; for example, a toy that primarily builds gross motor skills may also have some fine motor features as well.) Traveling toys are those that are particularly portable or well-suited for places besides home.

I've included toys that also reflect the five types of play identified in "Which Toy For Which Child?" (see pages 90 and 141) by the Consumer Product Safety Commission: active play, manipulative play, make-believe play, creative play and learning play. I've also selected toys that help develop visual or auditory perception and skills, important precursors for reading readiness.

e also bath time toys in Chapter 5 (pages 47-49) and indoor eating toys in Chapter 6 (pages 58-62.)

GROSS MOTOR TOYS

"Ride-on toys" are a fun way to develop coordinated movement of the legs and feet. Charlie's favorite is the **Roaring Fire Engine**™ (No. 2016, $30 to $40) by Clover Toys, which comes with two "C" batteries to power the push button-operated,

realistic, dual-siren sounds and emergency light. (Don't worry, the siren sounds aren't too loud even for inside, which is where Charlie uses this toy.) To develop gross motor skills, this can be used both as a walker for young toddlers with its walker bar to steady new steps or as a ride-on. Charlie has also learned to use his fingers to press the button and to change the siren selection switch (which is numbered "1" and "2" for early number skills) and his auditory perception of the siren sound quickly became keen enough to identify real sirens that were even far away. With wonderfully realistic detailing, this ride-on has "sparked" a real interest in fire engines and trucks of all kinds. Clover makes equally exciting ride-ons with detailing and colors for both boy and girl toddlers. Also check out the **Roaring Choo Choo** (No. 2018) and **Little Miss Choo Choo** (No. 2101). (If you should see the "Li'l Fire Chief" in the store, it's identical to the "Roaring Fire Engine," except it has different packaging and doesn't come with batteries.) The Roaring Fire Engine is available at Toys R Us, Target and other nationwide retailers or call Clover Toys at **800/624-7775** (or in California, 714/994-1372).

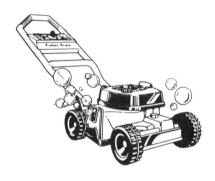

"Push toys" are real favorites with Charlie. His favorite outdoor one (although it's not a push toy per se) is the Fisher-Price® **Bubble Mower** (No. 2022, about $15). He first saw this wonderful, realistic, patented mower when we were visiting friends up in Sacramento and Baby Ryan had one. Although recommended for ages two to six, the mower has been fun for

Charlie since he was around 15 months. What Charlie especially likes is the realistic mowing motor-like sound that he can make easily by pushing the mower (no batteries required!) I think he also likes feeling big and powerful like a gardener (this mower is great for imaginative play). It also has a bubble making feature and comes with a four-ounce bottle of bubble solution. When Charlie is bigger, he'll be able to also "start the engine" by drawing out the pull cord starter.

Indoors, Charlie has enjoyed his Fisher-Price **Melody Push Chime** (No. 2018, about $9), which is recommended for ages one to three. He loves the pleasing chime sounds as he pushes this toy around the house. The biggest challenge for us as parents is insisting that it stay on the ground; when it's raised in the air, this plastic and metal toy is formidable indeed. M a j o r retailers such as Toys R Us, Wal-Mart, K-Mart and Target should carry both these Fisher-Price products or call Fisher-Price (New York) at **800/432-KIDS (800/432-5437)** for other stores near you.

Charlie also likes the sound of his Little Tikes® **Push About**™ **Popper** (No. 0010, $11 to $13). As the wheels turn, the large, clear cylinder rolls backward, causing balls to jump around inside with a gentle noise.

We have a set of the Little Tikes® **Garden Tools** (No. 4826, $10 to $13) that we keep inside, great for arm and hand movement and coordination with leg movement, too. Charlie loves to rake make-believe leaves as well as shovel and hoe make-believe dirt or sand. We'll soon be getting a set for outdoors especially since these tools are durable and made of bright, sun-resistant colors. Recommended ages are two to five.

I really like so many of the Little Tikes outdoor toys, that I've compiled my own "Little Tikes Wish List of Seven." On this list you'll find their new **Mini Van** (No. 4222, $75 to $90), shown on the next page, which is a two-door realistically-styled ride-on with cordless car phone, sunroof, wood-grain panels, dashboard and behind-the-seat storage area.

The Little Tikes® **Quiet Ride**™ **Wagon** (No. 4905, $50 to $65) is made of durable, double-wall, molded construction with soft, rounded corners and has a safe handle. It has high sides and a

back-supporting rear wall. Great for hauling big loads, this wagon also provides a stable, smooth ride (if your toddler convinces you to do the pulling). Recommended ages are 1½ and up.

The Little Tikes® **Airplane Teeter Totter** (No. 4180, $60 to $75) is an airplane-shaped teeter totter for one, two or three little pilots ages two to six. One toddler can ride in the cockpit

with its detailed instrument panel while the other two teeter up and down for a realistic fun activity. It also spins completely around and banks like a real airplane. It has a five-foot wingspan with easy-to-hold handles and a wide base for extra stability.

The Little Tikes® **Junior Activity Gym** (No. 4719, $80 to $100) is a compact gym for toddlers ages 1½ to four for outdoor (or indoor) play that Charlie enjoys at his "Mommy and Me" class. The platform creates a crawl-through tunnel or special hiding place. The panels, platform and slide are made of heavy duty construction with smooth, rounded corners and "slide lock" together easily without hardware.

I'm sure Charlie would love opening the four windows and the full-height door in the Little Tikes® **Country Cottage** (No. 4907, $220 to 250), not to mention all the make-believe domestic play he could imagine. The detailed interior has a sink with swivel faucet, a stove top with clicking dials and a push-button, cordless phone. It has easy lock-together assembly with no hardware. Recommended ages are two to six.

The Little Tikes® **Castle** (No. 4126, $250 to $299) for ages two to six is an authentic castle design that features realistic stone

facade and a tower with a platform. There's a secret hidden door behind the fireplace to crawl in and out of the castle plus a built-in slide for quick exits. The swinging front door has a latch and there's also a flag on a flagpole. Two views of the castle are shown above.

Be on the lookout for the new Little Tikes® **Island Cruiser**™ **Sandbox** (No. 4379, $75 to $90), which is a large sandbox in the shape of a boat that can hold 400 pounds of sand or can double as a wading pool. It has a weather-resistant hood with an easy-to-use handle that protects the sand against weather and pets. The durable steering wheel with large horn and clanging bell add to the play value of this product, designed for ages one to six.

All Little Tikes toys are at all major retail chain stores, toy discounters and small toy stores as well as the J.C. Penney catalog. You can also call Little Tikes (Ohio) at **800/321-0183** for local retailers. (I especially like Little Tikes toys since 95 percent of all their toys are U.S.-made.)

The Today's Kids award-winning **All Star Basketball®** (No.  960, about $35) is designed for ages two to 10 (with adjustable height) but even though he's not quite big enough, Charlie has had great fun testing out this wonderful product. Granted, he has to climb up onto the couch in order to do a "slam dunk" but that doesn't seem to bother him. Of course, he doesn't like climbing down to get the ball, so he usually asks us to get it. He's having fun practicing his ball handling skills with the realistic, though smaller, ball that's included. The Today's Kids patented basketball set comes with an exclusive breakaway rim that doubles as a place to store the ball. This set should be available at Toys R Us, K-Mart, Target and Service Merchandise or call Today's Kids (Arkansas) at **800/258-TOYS (800/258-8697)** for a store near you.

When we go shopping for a tricycle, the first one we plan to look at is the Playskool **1-2-3 Bike**™ (No. 50561 for boys, No. 50562 for girls, about $35). Winning a 1991 Parents' Choice Gold Award, this is a three-stage bike with training wheels. The first stage provides the stability of a tricycle. The final stage teaches a child to ride a two-wheeler with ease. Both the training wheels and the seat adjust to three different positions. Playskool products are available through mass merchandisers and other stores and you can call Playskool (Rhode Island) at **401/431-TOYS (401/431-8697)** for local store names.

FINE MOTOR TOYS

When Grandma Emily gave Charlie the Pockets of Learning **ABC Wallhanging** (about $30) for his first birthday, I never dreamed this decorative piece would become his first foray into the world of letters and words that start with those letters. I hung the wall hanging on a doorknob where it became a wonderful manipulative alphabet learning center. He was soon learning letter names and names of the darling hand-sewn stuffed objects (called "pillow toys") that fit in the letter pockets. To be sure, his pronunciation was incomplete; usually he'd say only the first sound of a word. The ABC Wall Hanging was "voted best by kids" in *Woman's Day* Magazine. (The only down side to this otherwise exceptional product is to make sure your toddler doesn't put any of the small pillow toys into his or her mouth; if so, remove those toys, as we did with a couple of Charlie's pillow toys.) The ABC Wallhanging is available through the U.S. Toy Constructive Playthings catalog (Missouri) at **800/832-0572** and through baby and gift shops. You can also call Pockets of Learning (New York) at **800/635-2994** for local stores or to use their "Runaway Hotline" for lost or missing pillow toys.

The word of caution I just mentioned can apply to other toys in this section. Even though all of the toy parts would pass the Small Object Tester described on page 55 of Chapter 6, many may still be questionable for any toddler that's more interested in mouthing small parts than in using them for manipulative play. Supervise your toddler's play and instruct caregivers to do so as well. Be especially observant if you have older children in your home who play with toys that have small parts.

For a little more "ABC" learning, Charlie has really been enjoying the Fisher-Price® **Little People® School** (No. 2559, about

$25) which is loaded with lots of manipulative and imaginative

play for ages 1½ to five years. The door to the school opens and closes and the inside wall of the school is removable and becomes a puzzle with six "A-B-C" and "1-2-3" pieces. Six cardboard puzzle cards are also included. Charlie puts the Little People figures in the schoolhouse or outside in the play area where they go down the slide or on the teeter totter that goes round and round as well as up and down. There's also a miniature basketball game. Someone had fun designing this toy!

Another Fisher-Price self-contained activity toy Charlie enjoys
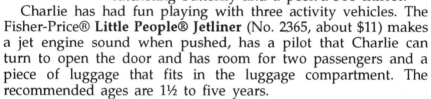
is the **Discovery Cottage** (No. 1030, about $22). Designed for ages 12 to 36 months, this patented cottage houses a jumbo Little People® figure and his dog who can take turns riding in the tricycle that wheels up a ramp into the garage, hiding behind the clicking front door or sleeping upstairs in the bedroom. There are also a rattling roller drum, a ringing door bell, a ratcheting butterfly and a peek-a-boo mirror.

Charlie has had fun playing with three activity vehicles. The Fisher-Price® **Little People® Jetliner** (No. 2365, about $11) makes a jet engine sound when pushed, has a pilot that Charlie can turn to open the door and has room for two passengers and a piece of luggage that fits in the luggage compartment. The recommended ages are 1½ to five years.

The Fisher-Price® **Kiddicraft® Shape Tipper** (No. 5618, about

$16) is a shape sorter dump truck with six colorful blocks that Charlie has tested and approved. (Introduce this truck after your toddler has mastered the circle, triangle and square on a simpler shape sorter such as the ones described on pages 101-02.) When pulled up, the dump handle makes a clickety sound, and it empties the pieces out to start again. Also a pull toy, the wheels make clickety sounds as it pulls along. (Be sure to trim the plastic cord to a safer six to 12 inches or it can be easily removed completely.) Recommended ages are 1½ to 4 years.

Charlie loved getting the Fisher-Price **Little People® School**

Bus (No. 2372, about $16) from his cousins, Doreen, Howard,

Brian and Jason. It comes with six Little People® figures and Lucky, the dog, and self-adhesive decals for bus detailing. When Charlie turns the driver, a stop sign swings out and the school bus door opens. He has fun taking the Little People on and off the bus as well as moving the bus around. Recommended ages are 1½ to five years. (For availability of Fisher-Price toys, see page 105.)

You can't go wrong with the Little Tikes **Toddle Tots®
School Bus** (No. 0800, $13 to $15) which is a wonderful vehicle for suggested ages of one to five years. It comes with a Toddle

Tots® bus driver and six Toddle Tots® school kids. The school bus roof serves as an easy-to-grip steering or carry handle, while allowing easy access to the passengers. The wheels produce a clicking sound as the bus is pushed and the stop sign pivots out to stop traffic.

I'm excited about all the Toddle Tots® toys. They are beautifully designed, quality toys that have smooth, rounded edges. Charlie

enjoys his **Toddle Tots® Dump Truck** (No. 0801, $11 to $14) with its two hard-hat clad construction workers. It was the first truck we bought for Charlie. I like the way the dumper tips easily to empty and the cab roof doubles as a large, easy-to-grasp handle for steering. The wheels produce a motor-like clicking sound. Recommended ages are one to five years.

We have been testing another Toddle Tots® toy set, the wonderful **Tikes Peak Road and Rail Set** (No. 0101, $35 to $45) for ages two to six. This is a set that's going to grow with Charlie, who's not yet old enough to understand the concept of putting down roads or track and leaving them there so that the train and car can use them. He's more interested in ripping up track just as fast as he or I can lay it down! The tunnel, however, with its peek-a-boo nature fascinates him. A great rainy day toy, it has endless play possibilities for both toddler and adult and will help Charlie with his small motor coordination,

make-believe play and eventually, social development. It's a 44-piece set that includes a large mountain with a tunnel roadway, a helicopter landing pad and two secret Toddle Tots® slides; a large two-piece drawbridge; five vehicles (a helicopter, a three-piece train and a car; 11 pieces of yellow road and 20 pieces of gray rail track (I like the use of two different colors because it's easier for toddlers, and parents as well, to spot color-coded pieces); three Toddle Tots friends; and two crossing gates. For Little Tikes toys, check major retailers as well as the J.C. Penney catalog or call **800/321-0183 (Ohio)** for local stores.

Charlie has enjoyed playing with toys that have many pieces or parts. (It's a good thing I'm a professional organizer because I have a natural tendency to help him keep those parts together with the right toy!)

One of his favorites (and ours) is the Little Tikes **Take-a-Turn™ Puzzle** (No. 0226, $11 to $13) for ages two to five years.

As Charlie learned his numbers one to 10 early, this combination puzzle and number learning toy (for numbers one to five) has special appeal for him. The toy can also be used for stenciling. There are also raised dots on each colorful number tag that correspond with each number. (For availability of Little Tikes toys, see Tikes Peak above.)

Charlie has enjoyed several Discovery Toys that are great fun as they combine fine motor skills with learning. One of our

favorites is the **Place and Trace® Puzzle** (No. 1750, about $13), which can be used in a variety of ways—as a puzzle, stencil, cookie cutter or a mix 'n match lotto game. It's an 18-piece collection of two-inch, colorful, detailed dinosaurs, zoo animals and transportation vehicles that store on three boards. Packaged in a durable storage box, the Place & Trace Puzzle also comes with a helpful educational suggestion booklet (as do most Discovery Toys). Charlie's visual and fine motor skills have really blossomed (and amazed us) with this toy. It's recommended for two years and up (but you may want to try this one earlier, as we have).

Discovery Toys makes a wonderful set of stacking and nesting cups called **Measure Up!® Cups** (No. 1640, about $10) for one

year and up. Several things set these cups apart. First, they come with a helpful guide that shows different ways to use the cups to explore size, sequence, volume and color. Second, they're purposefully only in four primary colors—red, blue, yellow and green—in order to simplify and reinforce the difficult concept of colors. Third, the cups are stamped with animal shapes on the outside and numbers on the inside. Fourth, they can be used later on to teach volume as the cups are proportional. For example, when you pour the contents from the first and second cups, it will equal the third cup; you'll fill the sixth cup if you combine the contents from the second and fourth cups, and so on.

A toy that's been a hit with everyone, even though it's suggested for three years and up, is Discovery Toys **Bright Builders** (No. 2290, about $19). Adults as well as kids seem to gravitate toward the bright, especially appealing colors and shape of these 24 3¼-inch star-shaped connectables. Even though Charlie can't physically put these pieces together yet, he still has fun handling them separately or handling the wonderful creations others make (and he will soon make himself).

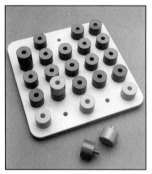

The 25 colorful plastic pegs in the Discovery Toys **Giant Pegboard**™ (No. 1650, about $13) are just the right size for Charlie's hands and so much fun for him to manipulate (as you can see in the back cover photo). Not only is Charlie developing fine motor coordination, he's also learning more about colors and patterns. The pegs easily fit in the pegboard holes and on top of each other. Charlie enjoys making tall towers out of the pegs. You can also string the pegs together (a shoelace works great for threading through the holes in each peg). The Giant Pegboard is suggested for age 18 months and up and has an extra set of 15 pegs you can buy for about $4.50. Call Discovery Toys (California) at **800/426-4777** for the name of your local "consultant" who personally shows and sells their toys.

Exploring the physical qualities of manipulative toys such as Bright Builders and Measure Up Cups occupies a good amount of Charlie's play time. He has also enjoyed the Fisher-Price® **Creative Pegboard** (No. 2042, about $17). Charlie can create an endless number of designs with this pegboard that features a unique "erase" activity. Charlie easily fits colorful geometric shapes onto the board and to erase designs, he just pulls a lever and all shapes drop off the board and into a storage drawer that holds all the pieces. Designed for ages two to six, the pegboard has parts that may be too small for toddlers who put them in their mouth.

Charlie has enjoyed the **Playskool® Letter Wood Blocks** (No. 214, about $4.35) set handed down to him by his cousins Lisa and Lora. These durable, sanded, nontoxic blocks for ages 1½ to five years have embossed letters on two sides and letters and numbers printed on the other four sides. They're great as blocks to stack and build as well as alphabet and number learning toys, for the toddler who's interested and ready. (For availability, see Playskool on page 108.)

Realistic toys become increasingly important for toddlers who are interested in make-believe play and everyday items adults use. Toddlers love TV remote control units, for example. I'm so glad we finally found a realistic substitute for the real one that Charlie has nearly destroyed with his mouthing and dropping. **The First Years Touch 'N Sound Toy TV Remote** (No. 2702, about $7) has red and green lights that flash with each tone, and each row of buttons makes a different exciting, electronic sound. Two "AAA" batteries are included and safely housed inside. Suggested for ages one year and up, this remote has buttons that may be a little difficult for some toddlers to depress at first (it's easier if you put the remote on the floor and have your toddler press down on the buttons, rather than having your toddler try to press the buttons while holding

the remote). An opening at the bottom is handy for attaching the remote to a stroller.

Charlie has had great fun testing out the award-winning **What's Cookin'** set (No. 1810, about $20) from Discovery Toys.

This realistic, quality-made set comes with a balance scale, hand mixer, rolling pin, pot with lid, pan, two bowls, mixing spoon, spatula and three cookie cutters. Charlie's had fun using this set with homemade clay dough as well as water. This set won a 1992 Parents' Choice Silver Award. (For availability, see Discovery Toys on page 113.)

Another way Charlie uses the set is with the Today's Kids **Magic Dishwasher™** (No. 830, about $32). This combination sink and dishwasher has a Magic Water Window™ that visually simulates real dishwasher action after Charlie turns the dial. The

moveable faucet really works with a refillable three-ounce water reservoir inside; as Charlie pushes down on the faucet, a small squirt comes out (there are over 500 squirts for controlled water play). Other features include a moveable dishwasher rack, retractable sprayer and soap-bubble wand. It's sturdy yet compact and portable. (For availability, see Today's Kids on page 107.)

TRAVELING TOYS

Besides books and tapes, which are great traveling pals and are described in the next chapter, I've come across some wonderful lightweight and/or compact toys.

Charlie loves his three Pockets of Learning handcrafted fabric activity toys that he plays with in the car (they're lightweight enough to toss in a travel bag, too). The **ABC Carrybag** (about $40) is a miniature version of the ABC Wallhanging (described on page 108) in the form of a handy zippered bag with handles. I appreciate the fine applique and embroidery detail in the ABC Carrybag.

Charlie is also enjoying **My Quiet Book** (about $30) by Pockets of Learning, which features wonderful toddler activities, such as buttoning, zipping, snapping and identifying colors, shapes and textures, in one handy quilted book. Call Pockets of Learning

(New York) at **800/635-2994** for catalogs that carry these specific products or local stores (which *may* carry these items).

A couple of cute soft toys also offer some of these same toddler activities. Charlie has enjoyed testing Fisher-Price's **Kiddicraft Dress & Count Clown** (No. 5756, about $17), which includes snapping, fastening, tying, buttoning, zipping and buckling. I like the numbers on the clown's hands to help with counting skills. For suggested ages of 1½ to five years, the clown is washer/dryer safe, too. (For availability, see Fisher-Price on page 105.)

I've also seen the **Dress-Me-Up™ Ernie** (No. 460, about $14) in the Playskool catalog. If your toddler enjoys Ernie on Sesame Street as much as Charlie, it looks like this washer/dryer safe dressing skills toy could be a great choice. It's for ages 1½ to four years.

Other Sesame Street soft friends by Playskool could also be a comforting choice especially on a trip to someplace new and different. *Be on the lookout for* **Touch'ems™ Sesame Street Pals** (No. 5366, about $11.20) and choose a squeaking Elmo, a crinkling Big Bird or a rattling Ernie. Each pal has seven special textures to touch and is washer/dryer safe (suggested ages are "from birth" but I'd wait until your toddler really recognizes and adores these characters). *Be also on the lookout for* **Sesame Street Babies** (No. 70220, about $17 each), which are baby versions of Big Bird, Elmo, Cookie Monster and Ernie and are suggested for ages 1½ and up. Also look for Playskool's **Sesame Street Hand Puppets** (No. 70448, about $16.25 each) for creative take-along fun.

For more take-along friends, the **Playskool® Animals** (No. 442, about $2.65 each), caught my eye in the Playskool catalog. There are twelve different realistically styled animals that are supposed to be easy for toddlers to handle. *Be on the lookout for* the new **Playskool® Horses** (No. 443, about $2.65 each), which include six beautifully detailed horses and the **Playskool® Dinosaurs** (No. 3100, about $2.65 each), which have nine dinosaurs with moveable heads or tails. All of these animals are for ages two and up.

Trips to the beach or the local park sandbox can be more fun with exciting toys, (although for us, the toys end up being more for the *other* kids because Charlie always prefers *their* toys). Here are some I plan to get for the "other kids." Playskool's **Sand**

Works™ (No. 1045, about $10 each) are two toys that scoop, spin, spill and sift sand. It comes with two sand-activated features (paddle wheel and twin buckets or spinner and dumper), chunky shovel and base with built-in sand castle mold, sifter and carry handle. All parts conveniently store in the base. For ages two and up, Sand Works parts are also interchangeable. (For availability, see Playskool on page 108.)

I also plan to get the Fisher-Price **Sand Kitchen** shown here (No. 2319, about $13), which is a seven-piece set that includes a sifter, beater, mixing bowl, muffin tray, double-sided play knife, spatula and cookie cutter, and the **Sand Workshop** (No. 2038, about $13), which include a brick mold, trowel, claw-hammer, drill and handy tool caddy. (See page 105 for availability of these two- to six-year-old toys.) See also page 47 for the Fisher-Price **Kiddicraft Play Buckets** and page 71 for the **Sandbox Sandbag**, a special tote bag for sand toys.

When Charlie was about four months, I discovered **Linky Rinks** (No. FOR-RL-21 with 21 links, about $8, other sets are

available) at a local toy store and considered them a real find. Previously called Rinky Links, they are colorful, durable, oblong plastic links that can be connected to form brightly colored chains or be used as manipulatives in learning. Each link has a locking and unlocking device that allows for ease of assembly and separation. Charlie loved to teethe on them. He used them in the stroller for teething and also for holding other stroller toys. A versatile toy that just received A Parents' Choice Expert Recommendation, Linky Rinks can be used later to teach numbers, colors and simple math. For numbers and colors, **Linky Rinks Creative Play Cards** (No. FOR-RLC, about $9) is ideal with its 14 special laminated number and color cards, or get **Linky Rinks Creative Play Cards Kit** (No. FOR-RLC-14, about $10) which includes the cards with 14 Linky Rinks. These two kits have suggested ages of three to six years, but some kids will probably enjoy them much earlier. I like the slogan of Forecees, the U.S. manufacturer, who believes that "learning should be a chain reaction!" Linky Rinks are available through The Right Start Catalog (California) at **800/548-8531**, the

Hand in Hand catalog (Maine) at **800/543-4343** or by calling Forecees (Michigan) at **616/649-2900** for names of educational catalogs or local stores.

Eden Music Makers (No. 00501, about $10 each) are wonderful lightweight, easy-to-hold musical toys to take along on outings or trips. The one Charlie has plays "Old MacDonald." It's a little difficult for Charlie to press and hit the right spot for the electronic melody to play, but Charlie never tires of me doing so! He loves this song, though, and can join in for part of it. Call Eden Toys (New York) at **212/947-4400** for local store names.

Century makes three wonderful soft, lightweight toys great for travel that we've had a chance to test. I loved the **Bag'N Train®** (No. 170-150, $25 to $30) as soon as I took it out of the box and so did Charlie. The train consists of three

fun activity bag "cars," that connect with Velcro® strips and can be detached, re-arranged or nested for extra play value. Charlie loves filling and emptying the cars as well as pulling them along with the safe-length pull cord. The big car has two roomy pockets for hiding special toddler treasures. The cars are washable and with their handles, they can be used as totes. The train activity is suggested for ages one year and up.

We're also having great fun with the Century **Kangaroo Playmates**™ (No. 170-159, $24 to $26). These cuddly mama and

baby kangaroo offer a variety of game playing activities. Baby Kangaroo becomes a hand puppet or doubles as a baseball mitt with Velcro® center for a game of catch. Three fabric balls and a mesh pouch develop mini-basketball skills. The Velcro® stars on the mama kangaroo's feet are also stick-on targets. It's ideal for parent/child interaction or take-along play. Suggested for ages two to five years, this toy has been fun for Charlie even though he doesn't have the ability to use it fully at his age.

Finally, consider one of the Century soft velour **Day Care Pets** (No. 170-152, puppy, which is shown here; No. 170-151, bunny at $14 to $16) for toddlers who go to day care or who have both parents away most of the day. The picture frame tummy holds

a comforting, family photo. The name tag insures the pet won't run away! A rear pouch can hold special treats and treasures. It's completely machine washable and suggested for ages 18 months and up. Call Century Products (Ohio) at **800/837-4044** for names of local retailers.

11

The Best
Tapes and Books

I've been looking forward to writing this chapter because music, pictures and words are such important parts of my life and I want you to know that it's never too soon to introduce them into your baby's life.

Because I started using tapes the moment we brought Charlie home from the hospital, I want to first share some of my favorite tapes.

TOUCHING AND FOOT-TAPPING TAPES

When we came home from the hospital, I took Charlie into the nursery, sat down on the couch we have there and cradled him in my arms. I asked Don to put in a new tape I had bought before going into the hospital. C-section notwithstanding, I looked into my newborn's face and listened to the most touching music I had ever heard and began to weep, even as I do now while writing.

Oh, sure, you could say I still had a lot of raging hormones going through my system while I was gazing down at our newborn and feeling awe over our own "private miracle" (as my dear mother-in-law Emily calls the experience of bringing a baby into the world). But the music truly was opening my heart to a new dimension.

We played the tape nonstop for days on our continuous playing tape player. It also carried us through the very special, though exhausting weeks ahead.

The tape is *A Child's Gift of Lullabies*® (about $13) by Someday Baby and is a multiple award-winner (National Library Association's "Notable Recording For Children" and a Grammy Awards finalist for "Best Recording For Children.") I learned about the awards when Someday Baby sent me their press kit. But perhaps the most powerful information they sent me were copies of more than 20 personal letters, almost all handwritten, by satisfied listeners. Never before have I cried reading testimonial letters but these were special, deeply personal letters describing how the tape had touched and transformed them and their loved ones. I related instantly to their emotional words about this tape, which is aptly subtitled "A collection of precious melodies and lyrics created with love and care for the young and old."

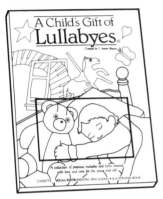

The packaging is precious, too, making this tape a super gift item (I've given it many times). And because I'm a singer, I appreciate the enclosed lyric booklet, which is beautifully done in full color. The tape is also available in Spanish.

Someday Baby has since come out with three other tapes. I'm especially excited about *The Rock-A-Bye Collection, Volume Two*, (about $13), which also was a Grammy Awards Finalist. *The Rock-A-Bye Collection, Volume One* (about $13), has won both the Grammy Award and the Parents' Choice Award. *Snuggle Up* is their latest lullaby tape. Call Someday Baby (Tennessee) at **615/385-0022** for local store and distribution information.

Many of the audio tapes in this section are in the soothing, lullaby category because our greatest need continues to be helping Charlie settle down and drift into sleep. We find music, along with other bedroom routines, have been very helpful for Charlie (and consequently, for us.) Times to Treasure has just released a unique lullaby set called **The Lullaby & Goodnight Sleepkit**™ (about $30 for Deluxe set, $15 for Mini set) we use that includes a music tape, bedtime story and parents' guide that helps parents introduce a whole bedtime routine for toddlers.

The audio cassette tape is called *Hush-A-Bye Dreamsongs* and features 12 fully-orchestrated original lullabies. Each side plays for

 38 minutes; one has vocals by Karen Carson and the other has instrumental versions. The hardcover book, *Goodnight Hands: A Bedtime Adventure*, is beautifully illustrated in full color and describes the story of a child preparing for sleeptime using his quilt, his fingers and his own vivid imagination. While the words may be too advanced for many toddlers, you can still use the exciting illustrations to make up your own stories with your toddler. The third component of The Lullaby & Goodnight Sleepkit is *Hush-A-Bye Know-How: A Parent's Guide to Sleeptime*, a useful booklet that explains why it's important to establish a bedtime ritual and suggests numerous ideas on how to creatively usher in the sandman. You'll discover the secret of using music, storytelling and games to make bedtime and sleeptime a fun, reassuring time. The guide also includes a complete bibliography of bedtime books, tapes and resources.

All in all, the Sleepkit is the only comprehensive educational tool of its kind available for today's families. The "Deluxe" gift-boxed set (about $30) includes the book, tape and guide. The "Mini" gift-boxed set includes the tape and guide for about $15. All items may be purchased separately without the packaging (the book is about $15, the tape is about $10 and the guide is about $3). For ordering information call Times to Treasure (California) at **818/591-1428**.

Music for Little People publishes (and distributes) two soothing audio tapes we use and enjoy. *G'Night Wolfgang* (about $10 for tape, $13 for CD) is a simple yet exquisite piano rendition by Ric Louchard of eight familiar, classical pieces that are natural lullabies by Mozart, Bach, Beethoven, Satie and Schumann. It was a nominee for the "Best Children's Recording Award" given by the National Association of Independent Record Distributors.

Lullaby Berceuse (about $10) is a beautiful award-winning tape (Parents' Choice Gold Award and American Library Association "Notable Children's Recording") that features lullabies in English on one side and lullabies in French on the other. As a singer and a former French major in college, I particularly enjoy singing along with this tape. There are some especially beautiful lullabies, lyrically and instrumentally (one of my favorites is "I Have You," which is very moving). Call Music For Little People (California) at **800/727-2233** to order these tapes, which you may also be able to find in a children's book and/or music store.

Alacazam! Records has a wonderful award-winning tape by gifted singer Priscilla Herdman we enjoy that is a combination of wind-down, sing-along "nightsongs" on Side One and an interesting selection of lullabies on Side Two. It's called *Stardreamer* (about $10; $12 for CD) and Herdman, who is also a mother, describes herself as a "song finder" who brings together "songs that deserve to be heard and have that special sparkle." Her voice and interpretations are special indeed. Winner of the Parents' Choice Gold Award and the American Library Association's "Notable Children's Recording Award," the tape is available through Alcazar mail order (Vermont) at **800/541-9904**.

I was first introduced to Discovery Music artist Joanie Bartels and her "Magic" tape series when I purchased her award-winning *Lullaby Magic* (about $10) when Charlie was very young. Bartels' voice, combined with the song selection and full orchestration on this and all the tapes in the Magic series, is truly "magical." Both *Lullaby Magic* and *Lullaby Magic II* are good, but my favorite is the first one, which has more traditional songs. Winner of the Gold Seal for Excellence by The Oppenheim Toy Portfolio, it also just received a gold record for over a half-million sales (Bartels is the first female children's entertainer to receive this honor).

Other favorites of mine include Bartels' *Morning Magic*, a great wake up tape that won The National Parenting Center Seal of Approval, *Traveling Magic*, which we use in the car, *Bathtime Magic* and *Dancin' Magic*, which is one of the happiest tapes I've ever heard that always gets Charlie and I moving on our feet.

Charlie, Don and I had the chance to watch Bartels in concert perform many of the songs from *Dancin' Magic*. What a treat! *Be on the lookout for* her first video, *Simply Magic*. After seeing her live, this is sure to be another well-deserved sensation. Discovery Music tapes are available in children's fine specialty and music stores and catalogs nationwide. You can also call Discovery Music (California) at **800/451-5175** for more information and a free catalog. A photograph of the tapes is on the next page.

For more foot-tapping tapes you'll also want to check out the music by the trio Parachute Express. This dynamic group combines original songwriting with lilting harmonies, gifted

musicianship and a real love for the music they create. With an uncommon blend of harmonics, their own unique contemporary sound and participatory, movement-oriented lyrics, Parachute Express brings a special joy to family music.

I first heard Parachute Express music at Charlie's Gymboree classes (see page 142). Their music was originally distributed by and created for the Gymboree Corporation. Parachute Express recently joined Walt Disney Records Music Box Artist Series label, although they will continue to support the valuable work of Gymboree.

They've done six albums to date (about $10 each for cassette, about $15 for CD). My favorites thus far (I haven't heard them all) are *Shakin' It, Happy to Be Here* and *Feel the Music* (which won a 1991 Parents' Choice Award). National stores that carry Parachute Express tapes include Musicland, Imaginarium, Sam Goody and The Disney Store. Also check with the Music For Little People catalog (California) at **800/727-2233** or Alcazar mail order (Vermont) at **800/541-9904**.

Charlie enjoys the music tapes we have by singer/song writer Raffi. Charlie's favorite is the classic *Baby Beluga* (about $11) distributed by

MCA Records, Inc. Many of Raffi's songs are participatory and all of the music, especially his own songs, reflect values that promote peaceful human interaction and a deep appreciation of nature. Raffi tapes are available through children's music and book stores and catalogs such as Music For Little People (California) at **800/727-2233**.

We've only just begun to see a few videos. I'm glad we've discovered a wonderful music video that has great participatory songs with movement called *Hap Palmer's Follow-Along Songs* (about $15) by Western Publishing Company. There are nine action songs acted out by young children with off-camera vocals by Hap Palmer (who wrote all the songs). Ideal for toddlers and preschoolers, this video is available through the Music for Little People catalog.

BEST BOOKS FOR BABES

Don and I didn't need much prompting when we discovered early on the importance of talking and reading to our infant. We're both published authors, so books have been a mainstay. We began reading to Charlie when he was a newborn baby. Imagine me sitting in front of a tiny infant propped up in his Graco swing as I read aloud books that were turned face out so he could see the pictures and there he was, actually showing some interest.

At the time of this writing, Charlie is 18 months and fortunately loves books (but then again, what choice does he have?!) He's more interested in turning the pages and looking at the pictures than in sitting down and listening down to an entire book. But he does come up to us frequently with a book of his choice and command us, "Read! Read!" We always try to physically or mentally involve him in "reading." I like to put him on my lap and ask him to turn the pages (which, by the way, he's done since he was about six months). I'll sometimes read some of the words and stop to ask some questions. I try to look for cues from him as to whether he wants me to read one page or the whole book or do something else altogether different.

It's not easy for me nor for Don to find good books for Charlie when we go to a bookstore (or the library). I can easily look at a dozen books and reject them all because they aren't appropriate or appealing. We look first for good, realistic pictures that use bright colors and aren't too abstract, "cute," complicated or cluttered. We also look for pictures and subjects to which

Charlie can relate (or potentially relate), such as everyday things he would see at home and outdoors. Books about animals, babies, other children, toys and vehicles are always good subjects for Charlie, as are those dealing with numbers, letters and colors (Charlie's interest in the last three has been sparked and reinforced by regularly watching Sesame Street, I'm quite sure.)

There should be simple text with only a few words on a page unless it's a rhyming book, which sounds more like a simple song anyway. If the pictures are great but the text is weak, you still may be able to get by if you're even the least bit creative by adding your own words.

We like activity books that involve Charlie with such things as lifting flaps for peek-a-boo surprises, touching different textures, naming things or counting objects. Charlie's participation is a key ingredient to making reading a thoroughly enjoyable experience.

Finally, our preference is strong, durable "board books" with laminated, round-edge, cardboard pages that ideally will take a large amount of toddler handling and mouthing. Even though most of Charlie's books have such construction, we have a portion of a shelf dedicated to "book repair," which is constantly in use! Stored in bins on the floor, most of Charlie's books are readily accessible to him. The few that are just too delicate are stored out of his reach. And now, onto our favorites!

The Putnam & Grosset Group
Many of our favorite books are published by this publishing group and should be available through your local book store.

One of the first books Charlie received as a gift from friends Dave and Marilyn was a Grosset & Dunlap Poke & Look™ Board Book called *One Green Frog* (about $10). I love everything about this sturdy, large-format, spiral-bound board book, which I've memorized after having read it so many times. The bright, appealing pictures by Carlo A. Michelini combine with clever die-cut openings for babies and toddlers to "poke and look" through as a rhyming, counting activity book unfolds. Written by Yvonne Hooker, this beloved book was one of the first objects Charlie was able to identify by crawling over to it when asked "Where's *One Green Frog*?" I think this book, along with Sesame Street, has played a major role in Charlie's interest in numbers, as well.

Two other favorite Poke & Look™ books are *What Does Baby See?* (about $10), which presents familiar objects in a baby's world and was written by Margo Lundell and illustrated by Roberta Pagnoni, and *Wheels Go Round* (also $10), whose author Yvonne Hooker presents a variety of different vehicles and the concept that they all have wheels. Toddlers interested in vehicles will probably enjoy the pictures by Carlo A. Michelini in *Wheels Go Round*. All Poke & Look board books have one especially nice feature: because of the spiral binding, you can easily fold over the book so that you can read the text on one side, while your baby or toddler sitting across from you looks at the picture on the reverse side.

Tuffy Tote Books™ with die-cut tote handles and Tuffy Tiny Books™ are other die-cut board books Charlie has enjoyed that present familiar objects and teach basic concepts. Written and illustrated by Tony Tallarico, our favorite is *Numbers* (about $4).

Pudgy Board Books™ (about $3) are small, charming books. It was fun to read *Who Says Quack?* to Charlie when he was quite young and attempt to mimic the various animal sounds in the book. The photographs and the text are well done and it was a pleasure to see him really enjoy this book. We've also enjoyed *The Wheels on the Bus* (illustrated by Jerry Smath), in large part because we've sung this popular song all the time in Mommy and Me classes, at Gymboree and at YMCA programs. We've just recently discovered *Guess Who I Love?* (written and illustrated by Mary Morgan) which is a very sweet book with excellent rhyming text, story and pictures that show how a little mouse finds special ways to show his mommy, daddy, baby sister, grandma and grandpa how much he loves them.

Spot's first words
Eric Hill

Of the "Spot" books, I really like the Little Spot Board Books™ for babies and young toddlers. Each of these books has its own unique die-cut curved right hand edge (as do the Pudgy Books) that makes them more interesting and friendly, along with simple, brightly colored illustrations by Eric Hill. The pages are laminated, too. Charlie has enjoyed *Spot's First Words* (about $4), which has clearly printed words for familiar objects and simple sentences using those words. It also looks a little like a reading primer that Charlie will be able to read by himself in a few years.

I picked up *Baby's Peek-A-Boo Album* ($11), written by Debra Meryl and illustrated by True Kelley, at an eclectic home store

called Bed, Bath and Beyond, which happens to carry different children's books from time to time. (You just never know when or where you'll discover a terrific book—be open to the possibilities!) This "lift-the-flap" activity book lets you and your baby or toddler play peek-a-boo with familiar people, pets and things. What's more you can customize the book by attaching your baby's pictures to the underside of each flap. You'll want to read this less-than-toddler-proof book together. Try not to get upset, however, when the inevitable flap is "broke," as Charlie says; just take it to book repair!

The Little Engine That Could (about $5) is a board book that simplifies and retells this classic story by Watty Piper, although it still has a little too much text for my taste. But the pictures by Cristina Ong are really wonderful and I also like the die-cut profile of the train that is cut out of three edges of the book. It's a sturdy, quality book with a laminated cover.

More Activity Books

A series of books by Merrybooks & More called *Hey, Look At Me!* lets you attach your child's picture to personalize them. You affix a photo of your child's face on the inside back cover so that the photo shows through the round hole that is die cut through the front cover and all the following pages. As you read each book, the text is on the left and on the right is an illustration that includes your child's face and illustrated body.

We have *Hey, Look At Me! Baby Days* (about $10), which chronicles such milestones as crawling, standing, sitting up, walking and self-feeding. For example, the walking page reads: "Hey, look at me! I can walk! I took my first step on_____." You can write in the date so the book doubles as a keepsake. The cover is laminated board and the pages are made of heavy paper stock. The book was written by Merry Thomasson and illustrated by Suanne Kelley Kopald. Call Merrybooks (Virginia) at **800/959-2665** to order this book or for a local store that carries it.

Western Publishing Company publishes two Golden® activity books Charlie has enjoyed. Dorothy Kunhardt's classic *Pat the Bunny* (about $7), which is more than 50 years old, simply asks the "reader" to perform a number of activities. The book's title, "Pat the Bunny," comes from the first activity, namely to pat the

fur that's in a cutout shape of a bunny. Charlie really enjoyed the peek-a-boo activity (he could lift the little square of gauze), feeling Daddy's scratchy beard, reading (and eventually tearing out) a miniature book, poking a finger through a cutout of Mommy's ring and waving bye, bye. This interactive book appeals to the senses—sight, touch and smell (there are flowers to smell, too). The suggested age range is nine months to three years (although Charlie was actively enjoying this book at about six or seven months). Since its first printing in 1940, Pat the Bunny has sold nearly five million copies. I only wish this book were a little more durable; Halina, the friend who gave it to us, said she had bought several replacement copies for her now grown children because they loved this less-than-durable little book so much.

When Charlie's grandparents Marilyn and Ralph gave him Western Publishing's Golden® Sound Story® book called *How to Get to Sesame Street* (about $22), which is for ages three and up, I thought that it was going to be too advanced for him. But I underestimated his interest in Sesame Street characters, vehicles and sounds. This is an electronic storybook with pictures of vehicles that each have a corresponding SoundPicture™ on a special panel to the right of the book. As you read the story and come to a vehicle picture, you (or your toddler) can press the SoundPicture to hear the realistic sound that vehicle makes. With ten different vehicles and sounds and 24 large format pages, there's a lot here to keep a toddler interested. Written by Liza Alexander and illustrated by Joe Mathieu, this Western Publishing Golden book is available at major retail outlet book and toy stores. (There are about 80 Golden Sound Story titles that vary in number of sounds and format.

We've found many vinyl activity books to be entertaining as well as durable. **The First Years Squeakie Playbook** series (No.  2309, about $3.15 each) has ten colorful pictures (and words) to help teach the names for familiar objects. Choose the fruits book (which Charlie has), the animals book or the vehicles book (not shown here), all of which have an easy-to-press squeaker built into one of the pages for extra auditory fun. The manufacturer's suggested age is "from three months."

Charlie has enjoyed **The First Years Activity Book** (No. 2319,  about $6), which has a mouse that Charlie or I can move through eight different slots or flaps. The mouse moves in and out of a swinging door to the house, sits on a chair to eat and sleeps in a little bed. He's also attached to the book by a short vinyl cord so that he doesn't run away. Another book features a bunny who rides different vehicles. Recommended for ages nine months to three years, these are also great travel books. For store locations, call The First Years/Kiddie Products (Massachusetts) at **800/533-6708.**

Charlie has also loved the Child Development Toys Program's vinyl activity books that feature a bear, a bunny and a kitty in everyday activities. Unfortunately, you can't buy these books separately; they're part of the Child Development Toys direct mail toy continuity program described on pages 93-94 of Chapter 9.

Simon & Schuster Favorites
Charlie loves two Simon & Schuster activity books, both of which require adult assistance for young toddlers. *Over in the Meadow* (about $13) is a pop-up counting rhyme (and song) that is beautifully illustrated by Michael Foreman, who makes birds fly, bees buzz and frogs jump right off the page when tabs are pulled and flaps lifted. I like to "sing" this book to the melody that Raffi uses for the same rhyming song that is on his *Baby Beluga* tape (see page 123 for more information about this tape). Suggested ages are two to four years for this book.

Charlie also adores *What's Inside?* (about $5), which is in the

Super Chubby® Lift-the-Flap Board Book series. I like the selection and clear illustrations by Eiko Ishikawa of familiar objects and the clever, simple rhyming text. The flaps in this book are more durable than most, too. Suggested ages are two to four years.

All the Chubby Books are generally durable except near the spine, right where the cover bends open. Baby teeth can easily puncture that area. We have reinforced our books with clear, two-inch wide, packing tape.

A Little Book of Numbers (about $3) is a wonderful way to begin introducing the concept of numbers. This is a Chubby Board Book with bright, simple pictures and snappy, rhyming text. Suggested ages are one to four years.

The Super Chubby Photo Board Books by Neil Ricklen feature adorable babies with everyday objects and in everyday settings. Our favorite book in this series is *Baby's Colors* (about $5) because it is so cleverly photographed. I like the clearly printed color words, too. Suggested ages are one to four. Simon & Schuster books are available at book stores nationwide or call their ordering number (New York) at **800/223-2336**.

More Concept Books

If a "concept book" (dealing with such things as colors, numbers and letters) is well done *and* holds your baby or toddler's attention, it's never too early to use them.

Harcourt Brace & Company publishes two of our favorites. Ellen Stoll Walsh's *Mouse Paint* (about $12 for hardcover, about $20 for a large-format softcover) is a charming color concept book that explores the adventures of three white mice who discover three primary-colored jars of paint—red, blue and yellow. This book has received critical acclaim (in our house as well as the real world).

We discovered Lois Ehlert's award-winning *Fish Eyes: A Book You Can Count On* (about $15 for hardcover and $5 for soft) in

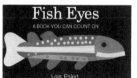

the library and soon realized this was a book to have in our own library. This is a clever rhyming counting book with extraordinarily bright colored fish whose eyes are die-cut holes. For ages two to six years, there is also a camouflaged introduction to basic addition for older children that doesn't get in the way of the main text and illustrations. Harcourt Brace books are available at bookstores nationwide or may be ordered directly from them (Missouri) at **800/543-1918**.

Our friends, Dina, Marc and Becca introduced us to the critically acclaimed *Jesse Bear, What Will You Wear?* (about $14)

published by Macmillan USA. Dina sings this book to Becca (who is two weeks older than Charlie) and now I sing it to Charlie. It's readable (as well as singable) with darling rhyming text by Nancy White Carlstrom and exceptional illustrations by Bruce Degen. Although suggested for three to six years, the book is wonderful for toddlers, who become increasingly interested in all the daily routines and activities of getting dressed, eating, playing and sleeping. There are two other books in the series but I haven't had a chance to see them yet.

Macmillan publishes another series of books called "Eye Openers," under the Aladdin Books imprint, that

once again appeals to toddlers as well as preschoolers. Charlie loves *Zoo Animals* (about $7), which features large, true-to-life photos, sturdy pages and big, bold type. The animals are presented against a white background, which creates a distinctive three-dimensional effect. This is a book that Charlie can grow with; as he gets older, he'll enjoy the simple, yet interesting explanations about each animal's habits. There are also close-ups of certain features for each animal. Macmillan Books are widely available through book stores nationwide.

As for the really strange concept of potty training, no book does a better job of explaining it to toddlers than *Once Upon a Potty* (about $5.50), which comes in "his" and "hers" versions for the book as well as the award-winning video (about $15) from Barron's Educational Series, Inc. Charlie enjoys his book about Joshua, who learns how to use a potty. For ages one to four years, *Once Upon a Potty* was written and illustrated by Alona Frankel and is available at bookstores. The toll-free number for Barron's (New York) is **800/645-3476**.

Random House publishes several concept books Charlie has enjoyed. Two are 100 percent cotton cloth books and are called *Baby Animals* (about $3) by John Parr and *Baby's First Picture*

Book (about $3.50) by George Ford. Both have good, clear illustrations and a small amount of type. Great for travel, these cloth books are nontoxic and washable.

Charlie and I really like two Random House "Chunky Books" (special square board books with 28 pages, which have a flexible binding with non-stick pages that makes them especially easy and fun for a baby to turn). *Baby's ABC* (about $3) with photos by Anita and Steve Shevett is a *great* alphabet book. (Believe it or not, great alphabet books aren't that easy to find). I like the selection of familiar items (rather than cute, esoteric things that might appeal to an adult). The photos are simple and uncluttered and each page also has the word as well as both the upper and lower case letter printed near the picture.

Bedtime Books

The concept of getting ready for bed and going to sleep isn't an easy one to master. Books can help teach that "concept" as well as help settle down toddlers before they go to sleep. Unfortunately, or maybe fortunately, books are stimulating, not relaxing for Charlie at this point. But such books are helpful for reinforcing the whole notion of bedtime.

I like to read Random House's board book *The Little Quiet Book* (about $3) in hushed tones not just at bedtime but whenever I want to create a quiet, calming mood. Katherine Ross's wonderful rhyming text combines so well with the darling pictures by Jean Hirashima. Charlie loves to handle the easy-to-turn pages by himself. Random House books are widely available through book stores.

 Of course, the classic bedtime book for toddlers is *Goodnight Moon* (about $12 for hardcover and $4 for soft) by Margaret Wise Brown and illustrated by Clement Hurd. The rhyming text (which Charlie is starting to repeat) and the fantasy bedroom that gets darker as the story proceeds help teach toddlers how to say "goodnight" to the world around them. Eden packages the softcover edition of the book with a soft, cuddly version of the main character, who is a rabbit in striped pajamas (No. 38015, about $22), which is shown here. I've seen this book/toy combination in local bookstores but call Eden (New York) at **212/947-4400** for retailers in your area.

Brita, a friend of ours, just gave Charlie another great bedtime book called *Maisy Goes to Bed* (about $13) by Lucy Cousins, published by Little, Brown & Company. Maisy the Mouse goes through her nightly bedtime preparations in a wonderful lift-the-flap book filled with delightful surprises for both toddler and adult. This book is available through book stores.

Charlie enjoys the **Musical Lullaby and Goodnight Book** (about $34) by Pockets of Learning nearly every night now. This is a wonderfully hand-crafted activity book that takes a bear with a musical tummy (press his tummy firmly and you'll hear Brahms "Lullaby and Goodnight" melody) through his nighttime routines. Sometimes, it's helpful, too, for sleepy parents who suddenly remember, when they see the bear's toothbrush, that their toddlers didn't brush their teeth! (But I'm sure that will never happen to you.) You can call Pockets of Learning (New York) at **800/635-2994** for names of catalogs or local stores.

MISCELLANY

I'd like to recommend one more little picture book that our friends Carol and Jon brought to us in the hospital, right after Charlie was born. It's called *Welcome, Little Baby* (about $14, trade hardcover edition, and $5, mini-book format by Tupelo Books). Written and illustrated by Aliki and published by Greenwillow Books/Wm. Morrow & Co., it's not only a wonderful welcoming gift (it was Charlie's first book), but it's great for showing toddlers more about babies, which they often find fascinating. (I always get such a kick out of seeing toddlers refer to "babies," when they were so recently babies themselves.) This is also a great book if you're expecting another baby and have toddlers or young children whom you can involve in welcoming the new baby.

Finally, here are my time-saving tips when shopping for books at book stores. Call a book store first before taking time to drive there and ask if a particular book is in stock. Have someone go check, while you're waiting on the phone, and pull it for you. If it's not in stock, ask how long it will take to get it and if the answer is a reasonable period of time you're willing to wait, then have the store order it for you, (unless it's a discount store, which may not do special orders). Ask to be called when it comes in (and also put a reminder to yourself in your calendar or planner). Remember you're under no obligation to actually buy the book if it doesn't meet your expectations.

12

The Best
Resources
For Parents

This chapter is a selection of the best parenting books, publications, videos, catalogs, keepsake/memorabilia helpers and organizations that I've found. (There are page references for any that were discussed in detail in previous chapters.) Also included are a few I plan to use sometime soon and wanted you to know about because I've read good things about them.

HELPFUL BOOKS, PUBLICATIONS AND VIDEOS
I have a favorite trilogy of books that I can't praise highly enough. I used them from pregnancy on through Charlie's first year. Published by Workman Publishing, they are written by Arlene Eisenberg, Heidi E. Murkoff and Sandee E. Hathaway, all mothers as well as medical writers who combine an empathetic, reassuring question and answer format with meticulous research.

When I was pregnant, I relied on their *What to Expect While You're Expecting* (about $11), a best-selling, month-by-month pregnancy guide and *What to Eat When You're Expecting* (about $9), which is particularly helpful for those of us who have experienced nausea and morning sickness.

What to Expect the First Year (about $13) was not only our "bible" but is another best-selling book they wrote that is highly respected by doctors as well. We read this month-by-month guide straight through and also used it as our main reference book, too. With every reprint (every two months or so) the What to Expect series is updated to reflect the latest medical knowledge. They are available at bookstores nationwide.

We also have relied on *Dr. Mom: A Guide to Baby and Child Care* (about $6) by pediatrician and mother Dr. Marianne Neifert (with Anne Rice and Nancy Dana). It's published by New American Library (Penguin Books USA). She, too, has a warm reassuring style with helpful anecdotes, backed by solid experience (she's also a mother with five kids).

If you're breastfeeding, I found the outstanding video series **"Breastfeeding Techniques That Work!™"** by Kittie Frantz, R.N., C.P.N.P. was extremely helpful and is something you'll want to have right away. (See Chapter 2, page 22.)

Cousin Maryl gave us a thoughtful, important gift called *A Sigh of Relief: The First-Aid Handbook for Childhood Emergencies* (about $16.50) by Martin Green. I really like the unique, quick-access index on the back cover and the hundreds of large, step-by-step illustrations with large type and simple step-by-step instructions. There's also a comprehensive prevention safety section that includes a handy checklist of first-aid supplies. Published by Bantam Books, this vital handbook should be available through most book stores. *Be on the lookout for* a completely revised and updated edition, available October, 1993, with over 100 new, two-color illustrations.

In addition, you should take an infant and child CPR (Cardio Pulmonary Resuscitation) course. As expectant parents, we took one with two of the expectant grandparents at a local hospital. It's easy however, to forget a lot of what you learned, especially in an emergency. I recommend, therefore, that you get an infant and child CPR video such as *How to Save Your Child's Life* (about $20), which features Elysa Markowitz, an American Red Cross certified CPR instructor. I like that this tape has both infant and child CPR. We watch it a few times a year and also have child caregivers watch it as well. It's available direct from the publisher, Xenon Video Inc. (California) at **310/451-5510** or they can provide names of retailers who carry it.

Quite early on, I found a wonderful little paperback at the market, oddly enough, called *How to Raise a Brighter Child* (about $5.50) by Joan Beck. I had known from my training as a teacher, that the first five or six years are developmentally critical. This book confirmed and expanded upon that idea, showing that parents can actually raise their children's lifelong level of intelligence and increase their joy in learning during this early period and beyond. Beck clearly explains scientific research findings and offers numerous ideas and activities to nourish the minds of babies, toddlers and preschoolers. Published by Simon & Schuster, it should be available through book stores.

I suggest you get a free copy of the "What Does a Baby See?" article by Ruth Wimmer-Ferguson, which is a fascinating, one-page summary of infant visual perception. Call Wimmer-Ferguson, Inc. (Colorado) at **800/747-2454** and see also pages 14-15 in Chapter 1.

I enthusiastically recommend you get a copy of *The Perfectly Safe® Home* ($10) by Jeanne Miller (also published by Simon & Schuster), which is discussed at length in Chapter 6, on page 51.

Be on the lookout for the next revised edition of *The Childwise Catalog: A Consumer Guide to Buying the Safest and Best Products for Your Children, Third Edition* (about $14) by Jack Gillis and Mary Ellen R. Fise and published by HarperCollins Publishers. Covering products for newborns through age five, this is an excellent reference book.

When your baby is nearing six months, get a copy of *Baby Let's Eat!* (about $9) by Rena Coyle, published by Workman Publishing, which is described in Chapter 4, page 39.

I'm planning to subscribe to the next two publications.

If you want to stay current on the newest books, toys, music, home videos, television programs, movies, computer programs and "all other materials affecting the imaginative life of children," subscribe to the quarterly nonprofit consumer newsletter *Parents' Choice* ($18 per year). The fourth quarter issue announces its annual **Parents' Choice Awards**, recognizing the year's best in each category of children's media. Almost all products have recommended ages, starting from birth on up. Selections are made by more than 400 people, including children. You'll also find recommended parenting books and catalogs. Besides the newsletter, Parents' Choice is a non-profit service organization that's involved in several other endeavors: literacy projects, special booklists, a children's video book and a press information service. To subscribe to the newsletter, write: Parents' Choice, PO Box 185, Waban, MA 02168.

The *Oppenheim Toy Portfolio* ($12 a year) is the only ad-free quarterly consumer review of the best toys, books and videos for kids from birth to age eight. Its concise, easy-to-use 24-page format is divided by age groups ("infants" are from birth to one year and "toddlers" are from one to three years) with separate book and video sections listing ages after each product. There's also a special feature called "Using Ordinary Toys with Special Needs Kids™," that highlights how mainstream toys can be easily adapted for use with special needs children. Each issue features their "Gold Seal Award" winners; the annual awards issue also includes three other awards, their top Platinum Award, their Blue-Chip Classic Award (for products that have stood the test of time) and the S.N.A.P. (Special Needs Adaptable Products) Award. To order with a Mastercard or VISA, call Oppenheim Toy Portfolio (New York) at **800/544-TOYS** or send a check to Oppenheim Toy Portfolio, 40 East 9th Street, 14M, New York, NY 10003.

One little book that's been very helpful thus far is *Potty Training Your Baby: A Practical Guide for Easier Toilet Training* (about $7) by Katie Van Pelt, published by Avery Publishing Group. This easy-to-read guide presents an early but non-pressured approach to potty training—starting as early as one year and perhaps completing it as early as two years. So far Charlie has made some positive progress (I'll let you know in the next edition how he finally does).

CATALOGS

I have used and recommend the first seven catalogs in this section. The last three I plan to use in the near future.

I have used the **Lillian Vernon®** and **Lilly's Kids®** catalogs for years. For children's products start with Lilly's Kids, although you'll also find some in the main Lillian Vernon catalog. Expect to find private label merchandise made exclusively for Lillian Vernon Corporation and specialty items you'll see nowhere else. Expect exceptionally reasonable prices plus excellent service and prompt shipping. Look also for their special sales catalogs—the offerings and savings are incredible. I buy a lot of gifts through these catalogs. To reach Lilly's Kids and Lillian Vernon catalogs (Virginia), call **804/430-5555**, fax at 804/427-7900 or write to Lillian Vernon Corporation, Virginia Beach, VA 23479-0002.

The slogan of **One Step Ahead™** is "thoughtfully selected products to help with baby...every step of the way." The focus is on functional, practical and educational products. You'll find child care products for babies and toddlers, as well as some educational toys. They offer free shipping if you order five or more items and very reasonable shipping rates for four items or less. To contact One Step Ahead (Illinois) call **800/274-8440** or fax them at 708/615-2162. For questions about products or services call 800/950-5120.

If you've read Chapter 6, then you know how much I like the **Perfectly Safe® Catalog** (Ohio) that focuses on baby proofing and safety products. See page 51 in Chapter 6 or call **800/837-KIDS (800/837-5437)** for a catalog.

On the cutting edge of infant and toddler products, **The Right Start Catalog**, prides itself on continually introducing new  products in the baby industry. You'll see special easy-to-spot "What's New" products on practically every other page. It's a pleasure to go through this award-winning (*Parents' Choice* has approved it for the last three consecutive years), well-designed catalog that is laid out and organized so well. It includes a wide assortment of about 300 unique products aimed at making parenting more convenient and fulfilling. Every product is pre-tested for safety, design and value and as a result, the catalog offers an unconditional guarantee of satisfaction (a guarantee that appears right on the cover). Their toll-free, 24-hour, order and customer service number (California) is **800/LITTLE 1 (800/548-8531)**.

Music For Little People is another award-winning catalog that's been approved by *Parents' Choice* for the last three years. Specializing in music tapes, CDs and videos that are "nonviolent, nonsexist, multicultural and environmentally sensitive," this catalog also has its own recording labels with many award winners. It's a pleasure to call this company, whose staff are always helpful and obviously enjoy what they do. Their number (California) is **800/346-4445** or fax them at 707/923-3991.

The **Bringing Up Baby** catalog is really part catalog and part newsletter. The catalog not only offers special quality products, it also shares important information and parenting tips. I trust the experience of Corky Harvey and Wendy Haldeman, the creators of this friendly, personal catalog. Harvey and Haldeman are RNs, childbirth educators and lactation consultants who work extensively with expectant parents, newborn infants and nursing mothers. Call Bringing Up Baby (California) at **310/826-5774**.

Three other catalogs look like ones I'm going to use soon. **Gryphon House Early Childhood Books** (Maryland) is *Parents' Choice* approved, offering hundreds of books for children six months to eight years. The number is **800/638-0928**.

Hand in Hand is a beautifully-designed catalog that features practical and fun products for young children, including toddlers, and their families. A typical catalog offers 400 products, including strollers, furniture, videos, books, housewares, safety products, toys and travel products. I like the handy table of contents with page numbers at the beginning of the catalog. Call **800/872-9745** (Maine) for a catalog.

Close to press time, I heard about a unique, exciting catalog and membership club called **The Baby Club of America** (the one-time membership fee of $25 includes free associate membership for up to five family members or friends). The Baby Club was formed to help parents overcome some of today's problems in raising small children (pre-natal through age three).

The catalog combines the convenience of catalog shopping with the pricing advantage of a discount club. It offers a full array of products, from hard to find and unusual to the basic necessities, at discounted prices for members. (I noticed that the catalog has many of the products from *Baby's Best!*) Once an order is received, The Baby Club will ship in-stock merchandise the same day.

Other member benefits and services include: a guaranteed lowest price policy; a baby shower registry (all shower guests may buy at member prices); birth announcement mailing service; home delivery of 30 baby care items (for example, formula, diapers and baby wipes) with no delivery charge, although these items are at normal grocery store prices; a quarterly newsletter with health and safety articles as well as a total listing of product recalls and retrofit announcements and special "Alertgrams" sent between newsletters that alert members to newsworthy information of critical importance; and special member-exclusive sales and closeouts. All in all, it looks like The Baby Club is helping parents, especially first-time parents, save some money and make life a little easier and more convenient. Contact The Baby Club of America (Connecticut) at **800/PLAYPEN (800/752-9736)**.

ORGANIZATIONS AND MORE PUBLICATIONS

These are organizations and publications I've either used personally and/or have consulted in the writing of this book. The **Juvenile Products Manufacturers Association (JPMA)** is a national trade organization of over 250 juvenile products manufacturers in the U.S. and Canada, representing 95 percent of the industry. A primary goal of JPMA is to develop consumer education and product safety programs.

Throughout *Baby's Best!*, I've referred to the JPMA Safety Certification Program. JPMA initiated this important program in 1976 with the help of consumers and Consumer Product Safety Commission representatives and implemented it under the auspices of the American Society of Testing and Material (ASTM), which is a highly respected nonprofit organization that publishes standards for materials, products, systems and services. To date, nine categories of products can be certified: high chairs, gates, enclosures, carriages, strollers, portable hook-on chairs, play yards, walkers and full-size cribs. Since JPMA launched its certification program, hundreds of product line models in these categories have been certified.

Special standards and tests have been designed for products in these nine categories because these are basic products that are used often—and strenuously. In the future, standards may be developed for other product categories so that they may be "JPMA Certified," too. To become JPMA Certified, a product must

be tested by an independent testing facility for compliance with the specific ASTM standards. If a product passes the tests, JPMA allows the manufacturer to label it with a JPMA Certified mark (see example shown here). Look for this mark on a product or its package. If you're interested in a product, but are unsure whether it has been JPMA Certified, ask your retailer for assistance or call the manufacturer.

To get the new JPMA guide, "**Safe and Sound For Baby**," a 16-page booklet on baby product safety, use and selection, send a stamped, self-addressed, business-size envelope to: JPMA, Two Greentree Centre, PO Box 955, Marlton, NJ 08053. (Their phone number is 609/985-2878.)

The **Consumer Product Safety Commission (CPSC)** is an independent, regulatory U.S. government agency whose mission is to protect consumers from unsafe products. They are able to order recalls, ban products and set mandatory safety standards and labeling requirements for products. You can contact them in writing or through their hotline to report a product hazard or a product-related injury.

In addition, they publish many free consumer safety publications of special interest to parents. I discussed No. 285, **"Which Toy For Which Child: A Consumer's Guide to Selecting Suitable Toys, Ages Birth Through Five"** in Chapter 9 on page 90. Also helpful is No. 281, **"For Kids' Sake, Think Toy Safety,"** and No. 200 (and 200S in Spanish), **"Tips For Your Baby's Safety."** To request these booklets or a listing of their other publications, write to: Publication Request, CPSC, Washington, DC 20207. To get information about recalls (except for baby car seats, which aren't under the jurisdiction of CPSC, see NHTSA below) or to file a complaint about an unsafe product call the hotline at **800/638-CPSC (800/638-2772).** A teletypewriter for the deaf is available on 800/638-8270 or in Maryland, 800/492-8104.

SafetyBeltSafe U.S.A. is the only national organization focusing on child passenger safety as its main objective. It offers a toll-free hotline, educational workshops, speakers bureau, an audio-visual library and an outstanding bi-monthly newsletter. Besides knowing the latest car seat recalls, the organization is working hard on such issues as safety belts on school buses (which unbelievably is *not* a law yet), increased safety for children on airplanes and the importance of shoulder belt use in all vehicles. Their hotline number is **800/745-SAFE** (or 310/673-2666 in Los Angeles.) For more information, see pages 71-74 in Chapter 7.

The **National Highway Traffic Safety Administration (NHTSA)** was established as an agency of the U.S. Department of Transportation to carry out safety and consumer programs. NHTSA's highest priority is to reduce deaths, injuries and economic losses from motor vehicle crashes. To improve highway safety the agency conducts balanced programs to promote both safer vehicles and safer driving practices. NHTSA sets and enforces federal safety standards for new motor vehicles of all types, investigates alleged safety defects and orders recalls where necessary, and conducts extensive research on ways to improve vehicle safety. You can use their toll-free Auto Safety Hotline to report a safety problem or to receive information such as **"The Child Safety Seat Recall"** package by calling **800/424-9393** (or **202/366-0123** in the Washington, DC area). Their address is: NHTSA, 400 Seventh Street, SW, NTS-ll, Washington, DC 20590.

The **National Parenting Center** (TNPC) is an advice and information service covering the entire spectrum of child care in seven age categories: pregnancy, newborn, infant, toddler, pre-school, pre-teen and adolescent. TNPC also conducts its own bi-annual **Seal of Approval** awards program that recognizes products that enhance, educate and contribute to the advancement of positive parenting and effective child rearing. The Seal honors books, videos, toys, children's furniture and accessories, along with new products such as computer programs, safety items and the like.

TNPC subscribers can get information by phone or computer (the latter through the Prodigy Service). Members also get a monthly newsletter called *ParentTalk*, brochures by TNPC specialists, discounts on books and videos and their bi-annual "Seal of Approval Report." Membership cost is about $20 a year. For more information (or to subscribe with a credit card) call **800/753-6667**. (Their address is 22801 Ventura Blvd., Suite 110, Woodland Hills, CA 91367.)

For sheer enjoyment and fun interaction between parent and baby or toddler, I recommend the **Gymboree Play Program**, which currently operates more than 300 locations worldwide. There are 45-minute classes for newborns through five-year-olds (seven different levels). We never quite made it to the newborns to three months class, "CradleGym™" (I was too sleep deprived), but Charlie, Don and I have gone to "BabyGym" (three to 12 months), "Gymboree I" (10 to 16 months) and "Gymboree II" (12 to 30 months).

At Gymboree, Charlie uses their durable, padded, brightly-colored play equipment, "socializes" with kids his own age and participates in imaginative group activities and singing. Most of the trained leaders are terrific. It's a well-designed program that is developmentally age appropriate. There should be a local Gymboree Play Program number in your phone book; if not, call the main number (California) at **415/579-0600**.

KEEPSAKES AND MEMORABILIA

If this is your first baby, you're probably going to take lots of pictures (and receive many cards you may want to keep). If you care about not only preserving your memories but also preserving your pictures and other memorabilia so that they don't yellow and age, consider "archival" or preservation photo albums, scrapbooks and storage materials.

My colleague Katy Chittick first introduced me to a company called **Creative Memories**, when she did a workshop for my chapter of the National Association of Professional Organizers. She displayed photo-safe albums, mounting products and album-making supplies. She also presented many creative techniques for arranging photos and memorabilia. (The sample pages here show how to combine photos with scrap book/journal techniques.) She also showed how many popular photo albums are actually destroying the very images they are intended to protect.

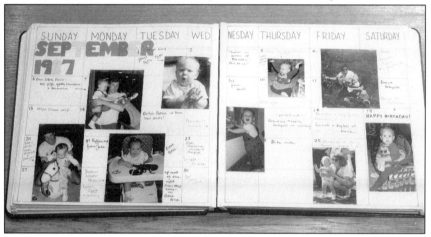

Creative Memories albums come with 30 pages of "acid-free," heavy-weight (80-pound), vellum paper and have a unique, patented, flexible binding that allows addition of many extra pages and provides for stress-free page-turning, keeping pages (and photos mounted on them) flat at all times.

Creative Memories offers a large selection of different albums as well as accessories, such as **plastic** mounting sleeves (made of photo-safe Melenex or polystyrene, *not* photo-damaging PVC), **Photo Splits** (which are fantastic, easy-to-use, self-dispensing adhesives I use to mount photos—they hold photos securely but allow for removal of pictures) and **acid-free pens**. Albums range in price from $18 to $38. The plastic mounting sleeves come in many sizes and styles. The handy **Picture Pocket Pages** ($7.50 for five sheets, 10 sides) hold photos in pockets without adhesive and are also perfect for storing a baby's hospital bracelet or first haircut locks. The Photo Splits are $3.75 for 500 count, enough for 125 photos. You can buy the pens, including calligraphy pens, individually for $2 or $12 for a set of six different colors. Contact Creative Memories, who may direct you to a local consultant,

by writing them at PO Box 1839, St. Cloud, MN 56302-1839.
For photos only, I use the 50-page **Heritage Album** with sheet protectors (No. 462-8511, about $56) from the "**University Products Archival Quality Materials**" catalog. The Heritage Album is an archival three-ring binder with a D-ring that lets the acid-free pages with sheet protectors lie flat when open. I use the Photo Splits on photos I put in this album, too. For extra pictures I'm storing that I don't wish to put in albums, I use their archival **Photo Organizer Storage Kit** (No. 180-756, about $18), which includes a cloth covered, hinged box, 13 photo organizer envelopes, 36 negative sleeves and one file index card. University Products also has acid-free notebooks (No. 678-0001, 5½ by 8½, about $4; No. 678-0002, 8½ by 11½, about $5) that we use to write journals about Charlie.

To save and preserve special fabric keepsakes such as your baby's first booties, a christening outfit or a special quilt or blanket, archival quality materials are necessary to insure that they reach the next generation unharmed. University Products has unbuffered **archival quality tissue paper** for padding such keepsakes as well as special **acid-free boxes**. Box No. 735-4118 (about $35) comes with tissue paper and is a roomy 41 by 18 by 10 inches, ideal for storing these keepsakes. Call University Products (Massachusetts) at **800/628-1912** or (800/336-4847 in Massachusetts) for a free catalog of these and other preservation products.

To preserve that special, first lock of hair, American Baby Concepts has a darling acrylic "frame" in the shape of a star or an apple. Called **First Lock of Hair** ($7.70 to $9.50), it comes with blue and pink ribbons, one of which you can use to tie together a lock of hair from your baby's first haircut. We plan to use it once we get up the nerve to have Charlie's adorable curls cut off. Call American Baby Concepts (Iowa) **800/537-7181** for a store near you.

And to record your baby's milestones, the book **Hey, Look At Me** (described on page 127) and the calendar **Baby's First Year** (described on pages 13-14) provide two easy ways to do it.

Baby's Best!
Gift Guide
A Selection of Products to Give as Gifts

The following is a *selected* listing of gift items organized by chapter subheadings and arranged by price within each subheading, starting with the most inexpensive (The few products without prices are at the end of a listing). You'll see a wide range of prices including some very inexpensive items included in chapters 3 to 11.

I've omitted products that you'd be unlikely to give as a gift. A breast pump, for example, is a highly personal product that a nursing mother would want to select for herself. On the other hand, I've included some breastfeeding pillows that would probably make excellent, thoughtful gifts and would be helpful to most nursing mothers.

On the following pages, you'll see the product name, the *approximate* price and then the page number(s) for further information. (And, as you can see from the back cover comments, *Baby's Best!* would make a great gift, too!)

CHAPTER 1: NEWBORN'S BEST

SLEEPING LIKE A BABY
Crib Light (Model 330, about $10), 7

CRIB BIB® (two to a package for **$16 to $18**), 5
Baby-Snuggleheads safety cushion (**$23 to $32**), 3
Baby Calmer™ (No. R12364, about **$30**), 4
Gerry Look 'N Listen Baby Monitor (Model 604, about **$40**), 6
Rock-A-Bye Bear® (about **$45**), 4
Tot Tenders Baby Carrier (about **$47**), 7
Dreamsheet Quick Change Bedding (**$50 to $60**), 5
Lamby Cuddle Rug (about **$60**), 3
Rock-A-Bye Bunny® (about **$60**), 4
Musical/Touch Lite Lamp (about **$75**), 6
Fisher-Price® Gentle Glide Bassinet (about **$100**), 2
Soothe 'n Snooze Bassinet (about **$169**), 2
Tabor Crib-n-Twin (No. 280, about **$649**), 6

IT'S CHANGING TIME AGAIN (AND AGAIN)
The First Years Wash 'N Dry Bag (No. 3105, about **$2.10**), 12
Safety 1st Wash'r Dry Bag (No. 156, about **$2.20**), 12
Safety 1st Baby's Own Laundry Bag (No. 252, about **$6**), 12
Bumkins Waterproof Tote Bag (about **$9**), 11
The First Years Nursery Organizer (No. 3111, about **$9.60**), 11
THE ORGANIZER™ by Prince Lionheart (about **$13**), 11
Fisher-Price® Diaper Pail (No. 9116, about **$18**), 12
Comfy Wipe Warmer by Rock-A-Bye Baby (about **$24**), 10
BUMP AROUND™ (**$30 to $37**), 8
Zojirushi Airpot (No. AALB-19, **$34**), 10
Zojirushi Airpot (No. AAB-22, about **$59**), 10
Bellini 3 Drawer Dressing Chest, Corso series, about **$599**), 8

MAKING THE MOST
OF THOSE PRECIOUS WAKEFUL MOMENTS
Pattern-Play (about **$13**), 14
Baby's First Year (about **$14**), 13
Pattern-Pals (about **$20**), 14
Century® Busy Bear™ **Activity Playmat** (**$20 to $22**), 17
Infant Stim-Mobile (about **$20** and **$26** with additional color
   cards), 14
Double-Feature scratch resistent safety mirror (about **$26.95**), 14
Summer Playtime Soft Seat™ (about **$30 to $35**), 15
Ruggie Bear® Activity Play Mat (**$30 to $35**), 17
Evenflo® Swing (No. 401166, about **$70**), 16

CHAPTER 2: NURSING AT ITS BEST

PILLOWS
Pregnancy Wedge, Model P-100 ($13 to $15), 20
Nurse Mate nursing pillow (about $36), 19

SPECIAL HELPERS
The Womanly Art of Breastfeeding (about $10), 23
Breastfeeding Techniques That Work!™ videos: "First Attach-
ment" (Volume 1), "First Attachment in Bed" (Volume 2) and
"Burping the Baby" (Volume 4), "First Attachment After
Cesarean" (Volume 3), "Successful Working Mothers"
(Volume 5), "Hand Expression" (Volume 6) and
"Supplemental Nursing System" (Volume 7), $40 each, 21

CHAPTER 3: THE BEST BOTTLES
AND ACCESSORIES

BOTTLE ACCESSORIES
The Bottle Burper® ($1.40 to $2), 26
Freehand® Bottle Holder (about $4), 26

WASHING AND STORAGE ACCESSORIES
NAP® Nipple and Pacifier Sanitizing Device (about $8.50), 28
SANI-STOR™ (about $9), 28
Bottle Dryer (about $12), 28
Fisher-Price® Bottle Organizer (No. 1520, about $15), 28
Easy Feedin'™ Nighttime Feeder™ (No. 3511, about $45), 30

CHAPTER 4: THE BEST MEALTIME MATES

HIGH CHAIRS
Fisher-Price® Deluxe High Chair (No. 9126, about $50), 32
Peg Perego High Chair/Youth Chair (No. 21-01-027, about
$119), 31
Home & Roam™ Double Duty High Chair (about $135), 32

Peg Perego Deluxe High Chair (No. 21-01-028, about **$139**), 31

BIBS
Bumkins Waterproof Bib (**$4** for regular, **$7** for junior), 33

MEALTIME FEEDING AND STORAGE ITEMS
Easy Grip® Fork and Spoon (No. 3035, about **$1.50**), 34
Soft Scoop Spoon™ (No. 3021, **$1.50**), 34
Scooper® Plate (No. 3068, about **$3.20**), 33
Scooper® Bowl (No. 3067, about **$3.20**), 33
The First Years® Sure-Grip Suction Bowl With Lid (No. 1625A, about **$3.30**), 34
Toddler Fork & Spoon (No. 1533, about **$4**), 34
Microwave Warm 'n Serve™ Dish (No. 3470, about **$4**), 34
Lillian Vernon flatware fork and spoon (about **$5**), 34
Lillian Vernon 40-inch-square vinyl mat (about **$10**), 34
Lillian Vernon four-piece dinnerware set (about **$15**), 34

CUPS
Cherubs Collection Training Cup (about **$3.20**), 35
Drip-less Cups (No. 3054, about **$3.80**), 36
Flow Control Cup (No. 1526, about **$4**), 35
Advanced MagMag™ Training Cup System (No. D775, about **$20**), 35

FOOD STORAGE
AND PREPARATION ACCESSORIES
Happy Baby® Deluxe Food Grinder With Tote (No. 800A, about **$12**), 36
UFO, Universal Food Organizer (No. 2001, about **$14**), 36

MISCELLANY
Baby Let's Eat! book (about **$9**), 39

CHAPTER 5: THE BEST BATH

EQUIPMENT AND ACCESSORIES
Safety 1st Bath Pal (No. 162, about **$3**), 42
SLIP-NOT MAT (No. 0590, **$5** to **$6**), 42

Safety 1st Swivel Bath Seat (No. 160, about $15), 42
Sinkadink, the Kid's Sink (about $15), 42
Fisher-Price® Bath Center (No. 9119, about $17), 40
Gerry® Two Years® Bath (No. 465, about $18), 41
My Potty Game (about $18), 43
Fisher-Price Soft Spray Tub (No. 9128, about $20), 41
Century 4-Way Potty Trainer (No. 9660, $25 to $30), 42
Polliwog™ Bathtub Sidewall Cushion (about $30), 41
Bathe & Change (about $438), 41

TOWELS
Li'l Hoodl'ems™ Hooded Towel ($7 to $8), 44
Kid Kaper® towel ($15 to $17), 44
Basic Easy Dry (No. BA600), about $25, 43
Classic FancyDry® Hooded Towel (No. CL610, about $27), 43
Classic EasyDry® Baby Towel (No. CL600, about $29), 43
Bath, Bed'n'Beach Reversible, Hooded Robe ($30 to $35), 44

PERSONAL CARE PRODUCTS
Babycakes® ($2.50 to $2.75), 44
Un-Petroleum Jelly® (about $3 for a four-ounce jar), 45
The First Years Baby Scissors (No. 3201, about $3.35), 46
Baby Cream With Orchid Oil (about $3.60), 45
Nature's Second Skin (about $13), 45
Tom's of Maine Natural Baby Shampoo, 45

DENTAL CARE
Infa-Dent® Finger Toothbrush and Gum Massager (about $2),
46
The First Years My Own Toothbrush, No. 3210 (about $2.10),
46
Mr. Rogers First Experience Books: Going to the Dentist (about
$6), 47
MagMag Toothbrush System (about $8), 46
Tom's of Maine Natural Toothpaste for Children, 47

BATH TOYS
Play Buckets (No. 5606, about $7), 47
The First Years Stack'em Up Cups (No. 2311, about $7.20), 48
Captain Stack (No. 5677, about $8), 47
Busy Splash 'n Play™ (No. 5213, about $8.80), 49
Busy Bubble Maker™ (No. 5225, about $18.90), 49

Toddle Tots® Noah's Ark (No. 0011, **$19 to $23**), 48

CHAPTER 6: INDOORS AT ITS BEST

BABY PROOFING PRODUCTS

Safety 1st Small Object Tester (No. 126, about **$1**), 55
Flexible Door Stops (No. 76191, about **$1.70**), 55
Safety 1st® Oven Lock (No. 241, about **$2**), 54
Victor's Latch (about **$2.50**), 53
Door Knob Cover With Lock Guard (No. 76382, about **$2.70**), 54
Playskool® Baby Safe-Store Pail™ (about **$8**), 55
The First Years Nightlight with Socket Cover (No. 3517, about **$9.50**), 54
The Perfectly Safe® Home book (about **$10**), 51
Video Halt (about **$13**), 53
Gerry® Walk-Thru Gate (No. 545, about **$33**), 53
Superyard (No. 8634, about **$65**), 52

STORAGE ORGANIZERS

Keepers™ Snap Cases (No. 2281, about **$5**), 56
Keepers Stacking Bins (No. 3008, about **$7** each), 56
Super Size Toy Hammock (No. 805, about **$10**), 58
Keepers Window Bins (No. 2704 to 2706, about **$10 to $18**), 57
Keepers™ Clear Boxes (No. 2223, about **$15**) 56
Kids Cubes (No. 7004, about **$15**), 58
Selfix® Cubby Cubes (No. 7013, about **$20**), 58
Toy Hammock With Wall Hanging (No. 803, about **$25**), 58
Cart Wheels™ Bin Cart (No. 2428, about **$25**), 57

INDOOR SEATING
FOR SITTING, PLAYING AND NAPPING

Snuggle-Up™ (about **$17**), 59
Little Tikes® Rocking Horse (No. 4017, **$20 to $25**), 61
Boppy Lay and Play (**$20 to $30**), 59
Boppy "The Pillow Pal" (**$30 to $38**), 59
The Happy Napper (**$30 to $40**), 60
Today's Kids Play Table (No. 260NC, about **$32**), 61
Activity Rocker™ (No. 390, about **$35**), 61
Alpha Desk™ (No. 925, about **$40**), 61

Century® Kanga-Rocka-Roo® Plus (No. 12-489, about $71), 60
Graco Battery-Powered Carrier/Rocker Swing (No. 1301, about, $100), 60

TAKING THE STRAIN OUT OF PAIN
Safety 1st N'ICE BEAR (No. 143, about $2.50), 63
BumpBag™ from American Baby Concepts ($6 to $6.50), 63

MISCELLANY
Sleeper Keeper™ (about $30 for a twin size), 63

CHAPTER 7: THE BEST
ON-THE-GO PRODUCTS

STROLLERS
Peg Perego Amico, (No. 15-00-010, about $189), 66
CitiMini (about $276), 67
Tender (No. 15-19-200, about $309), 66
Aprica Newborn LX (about $370), 67

STROLLER ACCESSORIES
The First Years Attach-A-Toy (No. 3142, about $2), 68
The First Years Drink Link™ (No. 1112, about $2.45), 68
Rosie's Babies™ Stroller Netting by Diplomat (No. 704, about $4), 67
Snap & Go® Bottle Rings (No. 109, about $4.50), 69
Playskool® Baby Stroller Tray (about $9), 68
STROLLER SHIELD (No. 6401, $11 to $12), 68
Tag-Along Stroll-A-Bag (No. 1292, about $12.50), 69
LOVE BUG™ (No. 6701, $12 to $13), 67
Stroller Cover (No. 1102, $14 to $17), 69
STROLLER ACCESSORY BAR (No. 6500, about $17), 68

DIAPER BAGS AND OTHER TOTES
HOT + COOL BAG™ (No. 4201, $16 to $17), 71
Sandbox Sandbag, (No. 1002, about $18), 71
Aprica Tag-Along Belt Bag (about $20), 70
Cool 'n Carry Tote (No. R12363, about $22), 70

Babies' Alley® Original Multi-Pocket Nylon Traveler (No. 6700/1, about $25), 70
Duet Diaper Bag (about $70), 70

CAR TRAVEL
The First Years Car Child View Mirror (No. 3328, about $5), 75
Car-Go Bag (No. 158, about $7), 75
Baby Tri-pillow (No. BTP400, about $13), 74
Cozi Critters™ (about $18), 74
Rosie's Babies Deluxe Reversible Fabric/Terry Cloth Fits-All Seat Cover (No. 2912, about $18), 74

TRAVELING MEALS
Safety 1st Lil' Muncher Snack Box (No. 282, about $2.50), 75
Toddler Traveling Juice Cup (about $4.25), 77
The First Years® TumbleMates™ 4 Pack-A-Snack Cups (No. 1672, about $4.60), 75
änsa Sipper (about $5.25), 76
Toddler Tumbler (about $5.25), 77
Fisher-Price® Infant Dish, (No. 1527, about $7), 76
The First Years® Compact Food Grinder (No. 1029, about $10.80), 76
Evenflo® Snack & Play® The Neat Little Eat Seat™ (No. 290101, about $30), 77
Graco® Sport Tot-Loc® chair (No. 3045-29, about $42), 77

CHANGING TIME ON THE ROAD
Easy Change (about $110), 77

OUT IN PUBLIC HELPERS
Ride 'N Stride ($12 to $13), 79
CARTA-KID (about $20), 79
Tot Tether (about $30), 79

OTHER OVERNIGHT HELPERS
Travel Tub™ (No. 129, about $15), 80
Fisher-Price® 3-in-1 Travel Tender With Bassinet (No. 9156, about $120), 80

CHAPTER 8: THE BEST DRESSED BABY

FOOTWEAR
The First Years Comfy-Cuff Booties (No. 3701, about $2.10), 81
Padders® soft bootie/shoes ($7 to $10), 81

BEAUTIFUL BASICS
Funsie Onesies™ ($5 to $6), 83
Onesies® One-Piece Underwear, ($9 to $10 for a three-pack), 83
Healthtex Bodyshirt™ ($11 to $13), 85
Busy Body Jumpers ($17 to $25.50), 84
Traditional Shortall ($17.50 to $24.50), 84
Busy Body Shortalls ($18.50 to $23), 84
Traditional Bib Overall ($19.50 to $27.50), 84
Busy Body Bib Overalls ($19.50 to $25.50), 84
Healthtex Playwear Denims™, 85

ON-THE-GO ACCESSORIES
The First Years No Scratch Baby Mitts (No. 3700, two pairs about $3.50), 86
Baby Bumpers® knee pads (about $7), 87
Flap Happy® The Original Flap Hat (about $10), 86
Baby Optics Sunglasses (about $15), 86

OTHER ACCESSORIES
Uncle Randy's Baby Garters ($4 to $5), 88
Shirt Anchors (about $5), 87
False Bottoms garment extender (No. 1280 has two snaps, No. 1281 has three snaps, about $5.50 for two pairs), 88

CHAPTER 9: THE BEST TOYS FOR BABIES

CRIB TOYS
Fisher-Price® Big View Mirror (No. 1132, about $12), 92
Century® Cribanimals™ (No. 170-302, $14 to $16), 91
Barnyard Crib Center (No. 1533, $16 to $19), 91
Crib Rail Barnyard™ (No. 170-308, about $20), 91

Pansy Ellen Bright Starts™ Crib Mirror (about $20), 93
CribEssentials™ Mobile and Musical Crib Light (about $35), 90

FIRST TOYS
Fisher-Price® Activity Links Gym (No. 1090, about $25), 94
Today's Kids GymFinity™ (No. 330, about $34), 94

TEETHERS AND SMALL ACTIVITY TOYS
The First Years First Keys (No. 2049, about $1.55), 96
Happy Elephant™ Mirror Rattle (No. 76314, about $1.65), 97
Sea Shell™ Rattle (No. 76352, $1.80), 97
Circus Teethers (No. 149, about $2), 97
Shake 'N Spin Rattle (No. 76315, about $2.35), 97
Spinning Teether Rattle™ (No. 76304, about $2.40), 97
Baby Cassette Teether (No. 146, about $2.50), 97
Playskool® Click 'N Swirl Rattle (No. 5122, about $2.60), 97
Chime Rattle (No. 2129, about $3), 97
Fun 'n Fruity™ Teether (No. 3158, about $3.20), 97
Cow Bells Rattle (No. 1439, about $3.60), 97
Hide 'N Seek Rattle (No. 2115, about $4.10), 96
Soft Handled Teether Rattle (No. 2110, about $5), 96
Tons of Fun® Rattle (No. 1010, about $7), 96
Gummy Yummy (No. 1090, about $7), 96
Spin, Rattle 'N' Roll™ Activity Rattle (No. 1250, about $10), 96
Tumble Time (No. 1220, about $10), 96

TOYS FROM SIX MONTHS
Rock-A-Stack® rings (No. 1050, about $6), 101
Busy Camera (No. 5079, about $7), 98
TANGIBALL (No. 1340, about $9), 99
Baby's First Blocks (No. 1024, about $9), 101
Busy Guitar (No. 5131, about $9.25), 99
Rolling Reflections (No. 1140, about $15), 99
Play About™ House (No. 1518, $17 to $19), 98
Listen & Learn™ Nursery Rhymes Ball (about $25), 99
Activity Walker (No. 1040, about $30), 100

TOYS FROM NINE MONTHS
My First Puzzle (No. 2608, about $4.50), 102
Fit 'N Fill Discovery Pail (No. 2605, about $8.50), 102

Musical Shape & Sort™ (about $25), 101

CHAPTER 10: THE BEST TOYS FOR TODDLERS

GROSS MOTOR TOYS
Melody Push Chime (No. 2018, about $9), 105
Garden Tools (No. 4826, $10 to $13), 105
Push About™ Popper (No. 0010, $11 to $13), 105
Bubble Mower (No. 2022, about $15), 104
Roaring Fire Engine™ (No. 2016, $30 to $40), 104
Roaring Choo Choo (No. 2018, about $30 to $40), 104
Little Miss Choo Choo (No. 2101 about $30 to $40), 104
All Star Basketball® (No. 960, about $35), 107
1-2-3 Bike™ (No. 50561 for boys, No. 50562 for girls, about $35), 108
Quiet Ride™ Wagon (No. 4905, $50 to $65), 105
Airplane Teeter Totter (No. 4180, $60 to $75), 106
Mini Van (No. 4222, $75 to $90), 105
Island Cruiser™ Sandbox (No. 4379, $75 to $90), 107
Junior Activity Gym (No. 4719, $80 to $100), 106
Country Cottage (No. 4907, $220 to 250), 106
Castle (No. 4126, $250 to $299), 106

FINE MOTOR TOYS
Playskool® Letter Wood Blocks (No. 214, about $4.35), 113
The First Years Touch 'N Sound Toy TV Remote (No. 2702, about $7), 113
Measure Up!® Cups (No. 1640, about $10), 112
Little People® Jetliner (No. 2365, about $11), 109
Take-a-Turn™ Puzzle (No. 0226, $11 to $13), 111
Toddle Tots® Dump Truck (No. 0801, $11 to $14), 110
Place and Trace® Puzzle (No. 1750, about $13), 111
Giant Pegboard™ (No. 1650, about $13), 112
Toddle Tots® School Bus (No. 0800, $13 to $15), 110
Kiddicraft® Shape Tipper (No. 5618, about $16), 109
Little People® School Bus (No. 2372, about $16), 109
Creative Pegboard (No. 2042, about $17), 113
Bright Builders (No. 2290, about $19), 112

What's Cookin' set (No. 1810, about $20), 114
Discovery Cottage (No. 1030, about $22), 109
Little People® School (No. 2559, about $25), 108
ABC Wallhanging (about $30), 108
Magic Dishwasher™ (No. 830, about $32), 114
Tikes Peak Road and Rail Set (No. 0101, $35 to $45), 110

TRAVELING TOYS
Playskool® Animals (No. 442, about $2.65 each), 115
Playskool® Horses (No. 443, about $2.65 each), 115
Playskool® Dinosaurs (No. 3100, about $2.65 each), 115
Linky Rinks (No. FOR-RL-21 with 21 links, about $8), 116
Linky Rinks Creative Play Cards (No. FOR-RLC, about $9), 116
Linky Rinks Creative Play Cards Kit (No. FOR-RLC-14, about $10), 116
Sand Works™ (No. 1045, about $10 each), 115-16
Eden Music Makers (No. 00501, about $10 each), 117
Touch'ems™ Sesame Street Pals (No. 5366, about $11.20), 115
Sand Kitchen (No. 2319, about $13), 116
Sand Workshop (No. 2038, about $13), 116
Dress-Me-Up™ Ernie (No. 460, about $14), 115
Day Care Pets (No. 170-152, puppy; No. 170-151, bunny at $14 to $16), 117
Sesame Street Hand Puppets (No. 70448, about $16.25 each), 115
Sesame Street Babies (No. 70220, about $17 each), 115
Kiddicraft Dress & Count Clown (No. 5756, about $17), 115
Kangaroo Playmates™ (No. 170-159, $24 to $26), 117
Bag'N Train® (No. 170-150, $25 to $30), 117
My Quiet Book (about $30), 114
ABC Carrybag (about $40), 114

CHAPTER 11: THE BEST TAPES AND BOOKS

TOUCHING AND FOOT-TAPPING TAPES
Lullaby Magic, Lullaby Magic II, Morning Magic, Traveling Magic, Bathtime Magic and *Dancin' Magic* (about $10 each), 122
G'Night Wolfgang (about $10 for tape, $13 for CD), 121

Shakin' It, Happy to Be Here and *Feel the Music* (about $10 each for cassette, about $15 for CD), 123
Lullaby Berceuse (about $10), 121
Stardreamer (about $10; $12 for CD), 122
Baby Beluga (about $11), 123
A Child's Gift of Lullabies® (about $13), 120
The Rock-A-Bye Collection, Volume Two, (about $13), 120
The Rock-A-Bye Collection, Volume One (about $13), 120
Snuggle Up (about $13), 120
The Lullaby & Goodnight Sleepkit™ (about $15 for Mini set, $30 for Deluxe set), 120
Hap Palmer's Follow-Along Songs (about $15), 124

BEST BOOKS FOR BABES
Who Says Quack? (about $3), 126
The Wheels on the Bus (about $3), 126
Guess Who I Love? (about $3), 126
Numbers (about $4), 126
Spot's First Words (about $4), 126
The Little Engine That Could (about $5), 127
One Green Frog (about $10), 125
What Does Baby See? (about $10), 126
Wheels Go Round (also $10), 126
Baby's Peek-A-Boo Album (about $11), 126

MORE ACTIVITY BOOKS
A Little Book of Numbers (about $3), 130
The First Years Squeakie Playbook series (No. 2309, about $3.15 each), 129
What's Inside? (about $5), 129
Baby's Colors (about $5), 130
The First Years Activity Book (No. 2319, about $6), 129
Pat the Bunny (about $7), 127
Hey, Look At Me! Baby Days (about $10), 127
Over in the Meadow (about $13), 129
How to Get to Sesame Street (about $22), 128

MORE CONCEPT BOOKS
Baby Animals (about $3), 131
Baby's ABC (about $3), 132
Baby's First Picture Book (about $3.50), 131

Once Upon a Potty (about **$5.50**), which comes in "his" and "hers" versions for the book as well as a video (about **$15**), 131

Zoo Animals (about **$7**), 131

Mouse Paint (about **$12** for hardcover, about **$20** for a large-format softcover), 130

Jesse Bear, What Will You Wear? (about **$14**), 131

Fish Eyes: A Book You Can Count On (about **$15** for hardcover and **$5** for soft), 130

BEDTIME BOOKS

The Little Quiet Book (about **$3**), 132

Goodnight Moon (about **$12** for hardcover and **$4** for soft), 132

Maisy Goes to Bed (about **$13**), 133

Musical Lullaby and Goodnight Book (about **$34**), 133

MISCELLANY

Welcome, Little Baby (about **$14**, trade hardcover edition, and **$5**, mini-book format), 133

CHAPTER 12: THE BEST RESOURCES FOR PARENTS

HELPFUL BOOKS, PUBLICATIONS AND VIDEOS

How to Raise a Brighter Child (about **$5.50**), 135

Dr. Mom: A Guide to Baby and Child Care (about **$6**), 135

Potty Training Your Baby: A Practical Guide for Easier Toilet Training (about **$7**), 137

What to Eat When You're Expecting (about **$9**), 134

What to Expect While You're Expecting (about **$11**), 134

Oppenheim Toy Portfolio (**$12 a year**), 136

What to Expect the First Year (about **$13**), 134

The Childwise Catalog: A Consumer Guide to Buying the Safest and Best Products for Your Children, Third Edition (about **$14**), 136

A Sigh of Relief: The First-Aid Handbook for Childhood Emergencies (about **$16.50**), 135

Parents' Choice (**$18 a year**), 136

How to Save Your Child's Life (about **$20**), 135

ORGANIZATIONS AND MORE PUBLICATIONS
SafetyBelt Safe U.S.A. membership and newsletter ($10), 141
The National Parenting Center membership and newsletter ($20), 141-42

KEEPSAKES AND MEMORABILIA
First Lock of Hair ($7.70 to $9.50), 144
Photo Organizer Storage Kit (No. 180-756, about $18), 144
Creative Memories photo-safe albums (about $18 to 38), 143
Heritage Album with sheet protectors (No. 462-8511, about $56), 144

Appendix:
How to Contact
Companies and Organizations
Featured in *Baby's Best!*

The following is an alphabetical listing of companies and organizations featured in this book, including addresses and phone numbers. Each company or organization name and its main number are in bold for faster reference. (Also see the index entry for each of the following, which lists their featured products.) Space has been provided to the right of each entry for any notes you may want to make if you contact a company or organization.

Alacazam! Records
PO Box 429
Waterbury, VT 05676
800/541-9904
802/244-7845

Ameda/Egnell Corp.
765 Industrial Drive
Cary, IL 60013
800/323-8750
708/639-2900

American Baby Concepts
PO Box 217
Wheatland, IA 52777
800/537-7181

American Baby Products Corp.
5741 Clover Drive
Oakland, CA 94618
510/547-7714

änsa Company, Inc.
1200 S. Main, PO Box 2758
Muskogee, OK 74402
918/687-1664

Aprica Kassai USA, Inc.
1200 Howell Ave., PO Box 25408
Anaheim, CA 92825-5408
714/634-0402

Autumn Harp
61 Pine Street
Bristol, VT 05443
802/453-4807

Avery Publishing Group, Inc.
120 Old Broadway
Garden City Park, NY 11040
800/548-5757 or 516/741-2155

Babies' Alley
20 W. 33rd Street, 10th Floor
New York, NY 10001
212/563-1414

Baby Bjorn/Regal Lager Inc.
PO Box 70035
Marietta, GA 30007
800/593-5522
404/565-5522

The Baby Club of America, Inc.
719-721 Campbell Avenue
West Haven, CT 06516
800/PLAYPEN (800/752-9736)
203/931-7760

Baby Optics, Inc.
269 North Bluff
PO Box 1162
St. George, UT 84771
800/962-6874
801/673-8066

Baby Trend, Inc.
1928 W. Holt Avenue
Pomona, CA 91768
800/421-1902
714/469-1188

Bantam Books
666 Fifth Avenue
New York, NY 10103
800/223-6834 or 212/765-6500

Barron's Educational Series, Inc.
250 Wireless Blvd.
Hauppauge, NY 11788
800/645-3476
516/434-3311

Bellini Juvenile Designer Furniture
15 Engle Street, Ste. 302
Englewood, NJ 07631
800/332-2229
201/871-0370

Body Therapeutics, Inc.
12501 Philadelphia St., Ste. 102
Whittier, CA 90601-3935
310/945-8141

Bringing Up Baby, Inc.
12012 Wilshire Blvd., Ste. 105
Los Angeles, CA 90025
310/826-5774

Brite-Times, Inc.
15237 Sunset Blvd.
Pacific Palisades CA 90272
800/933-6393
310/454-9640

Bumkins Family Products
1945 East Watkins Street
Phoenix, AZ 85034
602/254-2626

Buster Brown Shoes
1950 Craig Road
St. Louis, MO 63146
800/225-4371, ext. 100
314/434-9553

Camp Kazoo, Ltd.
602 Park Point Drive, Ste. 150
Golden, CO 80401
303/526-2626

Carl's Wall Units
12400 Santa Monica Blvd.
Los Angeles, CA 90025
310/207-9964

Century Products Company
9600 Valley View Road
Macedonia, OH 44056
800/837-4044
216/468-2000

Children on the Go, Inc.
787 Glenn Avenue
Wheeling, IL 60090
800/537-2684

**Child Development Toys
from *Parents® Magazine***
Gruner & Jahr USA Publishing
685 Third Ave.
New York, NY 10017
800/678-2686
212/878-4507

Clover Toys, Inc.
16261 Phoebe Avenue
La Mirada, CA 90638
800/624-7775
714/994-1372

Confab Corp.
26300 La Alameda, Ste. 490
Mission Viejo, CA 92691
800/262-0042
714/348-9494

Cosco Inc. Juvenile Products Group
2525 State Street
Columbus, IN 47201
800/544-1108
812/372-0141

Creative Memories
2815 Clearwater Rd PO Box 1839
St. Cloud, MN 56302-1839

**Diplomat Juvenile Corp/Ecology
  Kids/Rosie's Babies**
25 Kay Fries Drive
Stony Point, NY 10980
800/247-9063
914/786-5552

Discovery Music
5554 Calhoun Avenue
Van Nuys, CA 91401
800/451-5175
818/782-7818

Discovery Toys, Inc.
2530 Arnold Drive
Martinez, CA 94553
800/426-4777
510/370-3400

Walt Disney Records
500 S. Buena Vista Street
Burbank, CA 91521-6715
818/559-6200

Earth's Best, Inc.
PO Box 887 Pond Lane
Middlebury, VT 05753
802/388-6500

Eden Toys, Inc.
112 West 34th Street, Ste 2208
New York, NY 10120-0083
212/947-4400

The Epicenter, Inc.
15 Bemis Road
Wellesley Hills, MA 02181
617/237-3333

Evenflo Juvenile Furniture Co., Inc
1801 Commerce Drive
Piqua OH 45356
800/233-5921

The First Years/Kiddie Products Inc.
One Kiddie Drive
Avon, MA 02322-1171
800/533-6708
617/588-1220

Fisher-Price, Inc.
636 Girard Avenue
East Aurora, NY 14052
800/432-KIDS (800/432-5437)
716/687-3000

166 *BABY'S BEST!*

Flap Happy, Inc.
3516 Centinela Avenue
Los Angeles, CA 90066
800/234-FLAP (800/234-3527)
310/398-FLAP (310/398-3527)

Forecees Co.
PO Box 153
Vicksburg, MI 49097
616/649-2900

Four Dee Products
6014 Lattimer
Houston, TX 77035
800/526-2594
713/728-0389

Geddes Productions
10546 McVine
Sunland, CA 91040
818/951-2809

Gerber Products Company
445 State Street
Fremont, MI 49413-0001
800/4-GERBER (800/443-7237)

Gerry Baby Products Company
12520 Grant Drive
Denver, CO 80241
800/525-2472
303/457-0926

Graco Children's Products
PO Box 100, Main Street
Elverson, PA 19520
800/345-4109
215/286-5951

Greenwillow Books/Wm. Morrow & Co.
1350 Avenue of the Americas
New York, NY 10019
800/843-9389 (201/227-7200 in New Jersey)

Gryphon House Early Childhood Books
PO Box 275
Mt. Rainier, MD 20712
800/638-0928

Gymboree Corporation
700 Airport Blvd., Ste. 200
Burlingame, CA 94010-1912
415/579-0600

Hand in Hand, Catalogue Center
Route 26
R.R. 1, Box 1425
Oxford, ME 04270
800/872-9745

Harcourt Brace & Company
Children's Book Division
1250 Sixth Avenue
San Diego, CA 92101
Customer Service: 800/543-1918 (Missouri)

HarperCollins Publishers
10 E. 53rd Street
New York, NY 10022
800/242-7737, 800/982-4377 (in PA)
212/207-7000

Healthtex, Inc.
2303 W. Meadowview Rd. Ste 200
Greensboro, NC 27407
800/554-7637
919/316-1000

Health Valley Foods, Inc.
16100 Foothill Blvd.
Irwindale, CA 91706-7811
800/423-4846
818/334-3241

Healthy Times
7364 El Cajon Blvd., Ste. 210
San Diego, CA 92115
619/464-1622

**Johnson & Johnson Consumer
    Products, Inc.**
199 Grandview Road
Skillman, NJ 08558-9418
800/526-3967

Judi's Originals
7722 E. Gray Road
Scottsdale, AZ 85260
800/421-9433
602/991-5885

**Juvenile Products Manufacturers
    Association (JPMA)**
PO Box 955
Marlton, NJ 08053
609/985-2878

La Leche League International
9616 Minneapolis Avenue
PO Box 1209
Franklin Park, IL 60131-8209
National Office: **708/455-7730**
Ordering: **708/451-1891**
Catalog: **800/LA LECHE (800/525-3243)**

Lamby Nursery Collection
305 Grover Street
Lynden, WA 98264
800/669-0527
206/354-6719

Lansinoh Laboratories
1670 Oak Ridge Turnpike
Oak Ridge, TN 37830
800/292-4794

Leachco, Inc.
PO Box 717
Ada, OK 74820
800/525-1050
405/436-1142

Lilly's Kids/Lillian Vernon Corp.
Attention: Order Department
Virginia Beach, VA 23479-0002
804/430-5555
Corporate Offices:
543 Main Street
New Rochelle, NY 10801
914/576-6400

Little, Brown & Company, Inc.
34 Beacon Street
Boston, MA 02108
800/343-9204
617/227-0730

The Little Tikes Company
2180 Barlow Road   PO Box 2277
Hudson, OH 44236-0877
800/321-0183
216/650-3000

Macmillan Children's Book Group
866 Third Avenue, 25th Floor
New York, NY 10022
800/323-7445
212/702-4300

Marran International
9808 Wilshire Blvd., Ste. 306
Beverly Hills, CA 90212
310/271-9911

Marshall Baby Products
A Division of Omron Healthcare, Inc.
300 Lakeview Parkway
Vernon Hills, IL 60061
800/634-4350
708/680-6200

The Maya Group
15621 Graham Street
Huntington Beach, CA 92649
714/898-0807

MCA Records
70 Universal City Plaza
Universal City, CA 91608
818/777-4000

Mead Johnson Nutritionals
Dept P-92
2400 W. Lloyd Expressway
Evansville, IN 47721
800/422-2902
812/429-5000

Medela, Inc.
4610 Prime Parkway   PO Box 660
McHenry, IL 60051
800/435-8316
815/363-1166

Merrybooks & More
1214 Rugby Road
Charlottesville, VA 22903
800/959-2665

Music For Little People
PO Box 1460
Redway, CA 95560
800/727-2233
707/923-3991

National Highway Traffic Safety Administration (NHTSA)
400 Seventh Street, SW, NTS-11
Washington, DC 20590
Hotline: **800/424-9393**
202/366-0123 (in Washington, DC, area)

The National Parenting Center
22801 Ventura Blvd., Suite 110
Woodland Hills, CA 91367
800/753-6667
818/225-8990

New Age Concepts
9574 Topanga Canyon Blvd.
Chatsworth, CA 91311
800/477-8009
818/999-5192

New American Library
(Penguin USA)
375 Hudson Street
New York, NY 10014
212/366-2000

The Newborne Co.
River Road
Worthington, MA 01098
800/237-1712
413/238-5551

North States Industries, Inc.
1200 Mendelssohn Ave., Ste.210
Minneapolis, MN 55427
612/541-9101

Nu-Tec Health Products, Inc.
390 Oak Ave., Ste. A
Carlsbad, CA 92008
619/720-2223

OFNA Baby Products
22600-D Lambert St., Ste. 1009
Lake Forest, CA 92630
714/586-2910

One Step Ahead
PO Box 517
Lake Bluff, IL 60044
800/274-8440

Only Natural, Inc.
14 Buchanan Road
Salem, MA 01970
508/745-9766

The Oppenheim Toy Portfolio, Inc.
40 East 9th Street
New York, NY 10003
212/598-0502

OshKosh B'Gosh, Inc.
112 Otter Avenue
PO Box 300
Oshkosh, WI 54902-0300
414/231-8800

Padders, Inc.
1000 Young Street, Ste. 310
Tonawanda, NY 14150
800/7-PADDERS (800/772-3337)

Pansy Ellen Products, Inc.
1245 Old Alpharetta Road
Alpharetta, GA 30202
404/751-0442

Parents' Choice
PO Box 185
Waban, MA 02168
617/965-5913

The Pearcy Company
03621 County Road 12/C
Bryan, OH 43506
419/636-4193

Peg Perego U.S.A., Inc.
3625 Independence Drive
Fort Wayne, IN 46808
219/484-3093

Perfectly Safe
7245 Whipple Avenue NW
North Canton, OH 44720
800/837-KIDS (800/837-5437)
216/494-2323

Playskool, A Division of Hasbro, Inc.
1027 Newport Avenue
PO Box 1059
Pawtucket, RI 02862-1059
401/431-TOYS (401/431-8697)

Playtex Family Products Corp.
700 Fairfield Ave PO Box 10064
Stamford, CT 06904
800/222-0453 (outside NJ)
800/624-0825 (in NJ)
203/356-8301

Pockets of Learning
31-G Union Ave.
Sudbury, MA 01776
800/635-2994
508/443-5808

Prince Lionheart
2421 S. Westgate Road
Santa Maria, CA 93455
800/544-1132 (outside CA)
805/922-2250 (in CA)

The Putnam & Grosset Group
200 Madison Avenue
New York, NY 10016
212/951-8700

Random House, Inc.
201 E. 50th Street
New York, NY 10022
800/726-0600

Red Calliope & Assoc. Inc.
13003 S. Figueroa St.
Los Angeles, CA 90061
310/516-6100

The Right Start, Inc.
Right Start Plaza
5334 Sterling Center Drive
Westlake Village, CA 91361
800/LITTLE-1 (800/548-8531)
818/707-7100

Rock-A-Bye Baby, Inc.
1404 SW 13 Court
Pompano Beach, FL 33069
800/762-5229
305/942-7990

Rubbermaid Inc.
1147 Akron Road
Wooster, OH 44691-6000
216/264-6464

Safe Care Products, Inc.
805 Wolfe Avenue
Cassopolis, MI 49031-0248
800/733-3004
616/445-2413

SafetyBeltSafe U.S.A
PO Box 553
Altadena, CA 91003
800/745-SAFE
310/673-2666

Safety 1st, Inc.
210 Boylston Street
Chestnut Hill, MA 02167
800/962-7233 (outside MA)
617/964-7744 (in MA)

Sandbox Industries
PO Box 477
Tenafly, NJ 07670
800/451-6636
201/567-5696

Selfix, Inc.
4501 W. 47th Street
Chicago, IL 60632
800/327-3534
312/890-1010

Simon & Schuster Consumer Group
15 Columbus Circle
New York, NY 10023
Information: **800/223-2348**
Ordering: **800/223-2336**

Sleeper Keeper
PO Box 10021
Newport Beach, CA 92660
714/262-1474

Smile Tote Inc.
12979 Culver Blvd.
Los Angeles, CA 90066
800/826-6130 (outside CA)
310/827-0156 (in CA)

Someday Baby, Inc/J. Aaron Brown &
   Associates, Inc.
1508 16th Avenue South
Nashville, TN 37212
615/385-0022

Stride Rite Children's Group, Inc.
Five Cambridge Center
Cambridge, MA 02142
800/662-9788
617/491-8800

Summer Infant Products, Inc.
33 Meeting Street
Cumberland, RI 02864
800/9BOUNCR (800/926-8627)
401/725-8286

Tabor Designs/Desta, Inc.
8220 W. 30th Court
Hialeah, FL 33016
800/822-6748
305/557-1481

Tender Moments, Inc.
1089 Oakland Trace
Atlanta, GA 30319
404/365-9090

Texas Instruments
Consumer Relations, PO Box 53
Lubbock, TX 79408
800/TI-CARES

Thermoscan Inc.
6295 Ferris Square, Suite G
San Diego, CA 92121
800/EAR-SCAN (800/327-7726)

Times to Treasure
22647 Ventura Blvd., #359
Los Angeles, CA 91364
818/591-1428

Today's Kids, Inc.
Highway 10 East
Booneville, AR 72927
800/258-TOYS (800/258-8697)

Tom's of Maine
Railroad Avenue
PO Box 710
Kennebunk, ME 04043
207/985-4961

Tot Tenders, Inc.
712 SW 3rd Street
Corvallis, OR 97333
800/634-6870
503/758-5458

University Products
517 Main Street
PO Box 101
Holyoke, MA 01041-0101
800/628-1912 (outside MA)
800/336-4847 (in MA)

**U.S. Consumer Product Safety
   Commission (CPSC)**
For publications write:
Publication Request
Washington, DC 20207
For consumer product problems:
800/638-CPSC (800/638-2772)
800/492-8104 (in Maryland)
800/638-8270 (has teletypewriter
   for hearing impaired)
301/504-0800

U.S. Mills, Inc.
395 Elliot Street
Newton Upper Falls, MA 02164
617/969-5400

Victor's Latch
PO Box 2164
Montauk, NY 11954
516/668-9249

Video Halt
714 Second Avenue
Troy, NY 12182
518/237-5246

Western Publishing Company, Inc.
1220 Mound Avenue
Racine, WI 53404
414/633-2431

Wimmer-Ferguson Child Products Inc
PO Box 100427
Denver, CO 80250
800/747-2454
303/733-0848

Workman Publishing
708 Broadway
New York, NY 10003
800/722-7202

Xenon Entertainment Group
211 Arizona Avenue
Santa Monica, CA 90401
310/451-5510

Zojirushi America Corp.
5628 Bandini Blvd.
Bell, CA 90201
800/733-6270
213/264-6270

About the Author

Susan Silver is a mother, teacher and nationally recognized organization expert who directs the Los Angeles management consulting firm **Positively Organized!** (*not* to be confused with *compulsively* organized!)

She is the author of ORGANIZED TO BE THE BEST! New Timesaving Ways to Simplify and Improve How You Work, an award-winning book that has more than 80,000 copies in print, was a main selection of numerous book clubs and is available through book stores.

With a Master of Arts degree in Education, Susan taught elementary school (grades K through 3) and also instructed fellow teachers in curriculum development at a California State University.

Today, she consults and speaks to businesses and individuals, helping them find better ways of working and living.

She has personally researched and selected the products described here in BABY'S BEST! and used most of them directly with her son, Charlie. Besides being good for babies, all of the products make parents' lives easier or more enriching. Her goal is that BABY'S BEST! will save parents time and money so that they can put their energy toward what they treasure most—their children.

A Personal Note
From the Author and Charlie

Helping *you* and other parents was the most important reason I had for writing this book. Charlie and I want to know if indeed *BABY'S BEST!* has been helpful.

We want to hear from you! Please write us in care of **Adams-Hall Publishing (PO Box 491002, Los Angeles, CA 90049)** with your thoughts about this book as well as any comments or suggestions for future editions. There's a simple, quick 'n easy form letter below that you can photocopy and mail. We promise to respond to your letter.

Future editions of *BABY'S BEST!* may feature your contributions (you, too, could be in print!). You'll see what products other parents are using to handle the challenges we all face.

Dear Susan and Charlie,

Here are some thoughts I have about BABY'S BEST!:

I like the following products—please list and tell why:

Next time include:

Please check one:
___ You can use my comments with my name in future editions of *Baby's Best!*
___ Please use this information anonymously.

Please print your name, address and phone number if you'd like to get a personal response back from Susan or Charlie:

THANK YOU!

Index

I've designed this index to be a handy, time-saving tool for you. You'll be able to find most every product by brand name, by type and by the company that makes or distributes it. Names of books and tapes are in italic type. You'll see many synonyms, subentries and cross references to help you easily locate items in a variety of ways. If you can't find a product in this index, it's probably not in this book!

A

ABC Carrybag, 114
ABC Wallhanging, 108
Activity gym, 94-95, 106
Activity Rocker™, 61
Activity Walker, 100
Advanced MagMag™ Training
  Cup System, 35
Ages
  appropriate, 39, 89-90
  suggested, xx, 96

Airplane Teeter Totter, 106
Alacazam! Records
  Stardreamer, 122
Aladdin Books, 131
All Star Basketball®, 107
Alpha Desk™, 61
Ameda/Egnell, 21-24
  Baby Calmer™, 4-5
  Breast Shell System, 23-24
  Cool 'n Carry™ Pump 'n Save
    System, 71
  Cool 'n Carry Tote, 70

Lact-E Lightweight Electric
    Piston Breast Pump, 21
Nursing Pads, 23
Nurture III Small Electric
    Breast Pump, 21
One-Hand Breast Pump, 21
American Baby Concepts
    BumpBag™, 63
False Bottoms garment
    extender, 88
First Lock of Hair, 144
Shirt Anchors, 87
Tag-Along Stroll-A-Bag, 66, 69
American Baby Products Corp.
    Uncle Randy's Baby Garters, 88
änsa® Company
    änsa® Baby Care® Infant
        Grip® Bottle, 27
    änsa® Easy-To-Hold® Bottle,
        27
änsa® Sipper, 76
Aprica Kassai USA, Inc.
    CitiMini, 67
    Duet Diaper Bag, 70
    Newborn LX, 67
    Tag-Along Belt Bag, 70
Arrowroot Cookies, 38
Attach-A-Toy, 68
Autumn Harp
    Un-Petroleum Jelly®, 45
Avery Publishing Group, Inc.
    Potty Training Your Baby, 43,
        137
Awards programs, xviii, 136, 137,
    140, 142

B

Babies' Alley® Original Multi-
    Pocket Nylon Traveler, 70
Baby Animals, 131-32
Baby Beluga, 123-24
Baby Bjorn/Regal Lager Inc.
    Bathe & Change, 41
    Easy Change, 77
Baby Bumpers® knee pads, 87
Babycakes®, 44
Baby Calmer™, 4
Baby Cassette Teether, 97
Baby Club of America, 4, 10, 14,
    43, 79, 139
Baby Cream With Orchid Oil, 45
Baby Let's Eat!, 39, 136

Baby monitors, 6
Baby Optics, Inc.
    Sunglasses, 86
Baby proofing products, 51-55
    appliance, 53-54
    cabinet, 54
    containers, lockable, 55, 57
    door, 54-55
    furniture, 51-52
    gate, security, 53
    locks and latches, 53-55
Baby's ABC, 132
Baby's Colors, 130
Baby's First Blocks, 101
Baby's First Picture Book, 131
Baby's First Year, 13-14, 144
Baby's Peek-A-Boo Album, 126-27
Baby-Snuggleheads, 3
Baby Tech™, 82
Baby Trend, Inc.
    Home & Roam™ Double Duty
        High Chair, 32
Baby Tri-pillow, 74
Baby wipes, 11
Bag'N Train®, 117
Bantam Books
    Sigh of Relief, 135
Barnyard Crib Center, 91-92
Barron's Educational Series, Inc.
    Once Upon a Potty book/video,
        131
Bartels, Joanie. See Discovery
    Music.
Basic Easy Dry, 43
Bassinets, 1-2, 80
Bath, Bed'n'Beach Reversible,
    Hooded Robe, 44
Bathe & Change, 41
Bath seat, 42
Bathtime Magic, 122
Bathtime Water Works, 49
Bath towels, 43-44
Bath toys, 47-49
Bathtubs, 40-41
Batteries, rechargeable, xxi, xxii
Bedtime
    books, 132-33
    routine, 120-21
    tapes, 120-22
Bellini Juvenile Designer
    Furniture, 5, 8-9, 62

Bellini 3 Drawer Dressing Chest, 8-9
Bib Overall, 83
Bibs, 33
Bike, 108
Bins, 56-57
Blocks, 101, 113
Body Therapeutics Pregnancy Wedge, 20
Books, 124-33. See also Gryphon House.
  activity, 126-30
  bedtime, 132-33
  board, 125 ff.
  cloth, 114-15, 131-33
  concept, 125-26, 129-32
  parenting, 134-37
  selecting, 124-25
  shopping for, 133
Booties, 81-82
Boppy Lay and Play, 59
Boppy "The Pillow Pal", 59
Bottle Burper®, 26
Bottle Dryer, 28-29
Bottles
  accessories for, 26-30, 68-69
  disposable, 26
  favorite, 27
  nipples and, 25-26
  nurser, 26
Bouncer seats, 15
Boxes, 56-57
Breast cups, 23
Breastfeeding, 18-24. See also Lactation consultants; La Leche League.
  pillows, 19-20
  products, 19-24
  pumps, 20-22
  sore nipples and, 23
Breastfeeding Techniques That Work!™ videos, 22, 135
Breast pump rental stations, 22
Breast pumps, 20-22
Breast Shell System, 23-24
Bright Builders, 112
Bringing Up Baby, 3, 8, 138-39
Brite-Times, Inc.
  INFLATE-A-POTTY, 78
Bubble Mower, 104-05
Bumkins
  Waterproof Bib, 33

Waterproof Tote Bag, 11-12
BUMP AROUND™, 8
BumpBag™, 63
Buster Brown Shoes
  Itty Bitty Busters™, 82
  My First Buster™, 82
Busy Body Bib Overalls, 84
Busy Body Jumpers, 84
Busy Body Shortalls, 84
Busy Bubble Maker™, 49
Busy Camera, 98-99
Busy Guitar, 99
Busy Splash 'n Play™, 49

C
Cabinet,
  locks and latches, 54
  toy, 57-58
Calendar, 13-14
Camp Kazoo, Ltd.
  Boppy Lay and Play, 59-60
  Boppy "Pillow Pal," 59
  Happy Napper, 60
Caps, bottle, 27
Captain Stack, 47
Car-Go Bag, 75
Carl's Wall Units, 57-58
Carriers
  car seats and, 72, 74
  front, 7-8
  swings and, 16, 60
Car seats, 71-74
CARTA-KID, 79
Cart Wheels™ Bin Cart, 57
Castle, 106-07
Catalogs, 137-40
Century Products Company
  Bag'N Train®, 117
  Busy Bear™ Activity Playmat, 17
  Cribanimals™, 91
  Crib Rail Barnyard™, 91-92
  Day Care Pets, 117-18
  4-Way Potty Trainer, 42
  Kanga-Rocka-Roo® Plus, 60
  Kangaroo Playmates™, 117
  Ruggie Bear® Activity Play Mat, 17
Cereals, 37-38
Certification, safety, 140. See also JPMA.
Changing pads, 8, 60, 70

Changing tables, 8-9, 41, 77-78
  products for, 8-13
Changing time on the road, 77-78
Cherubs Collection Training Cup,
  35
Chest of drawers. *See* Bellini.
Child Development Toys Program
  from *Parents® Magazine*, 48, 93-
  94
  activity books, 129
  Bathtime Water Works, 49
  Red Rings, 94
  Ship Shape Village, 48
  Tracking Tube, 93-93
  Wiggle Worm, 94
Child proofing. *See* Baby proofing.
Children on the Go
  Folding Potty Seat, 78
  Snap & Go® Bottle Rings, 69
  Stroller Umbrella, 69
"Child Safety Seat Recall" package,
  141
Child's Gift of Lullabies®, 120
Childwise Catalog, 136
Chime Rattle, 97
Chubby Board Books, 130
Chunky Books, 132
Circus Teethers, 97
CitiMini, 67
Classic EasyDry® Baby Towel, 43
Classic FancyDry® Hooded Towel,
  43
Closet organizers, 58
Clothes, 81-88
Clothing accessories, 86-88
Clover Toys, Inc.
  Little Miss Choo Choo, 104
  Roaring Choo Choo, 104
  Roaring Fire Engine™, 104
Cold packs, 63
Collars, bottle, 27
Comforters, 17
Comfy Wipe Warmer, 10
Confab Corp.
  NewDay's Choice Baby Wipes,
  11
Consumer Product Safety
  Commission. *See* CPSC.
Cookies, 38-39
Cool 'n Carry™ Pump 'n Save
  System, 71
Cool 'n Carry Tote, 70

Cosco Inc. Juvenile Products
  Group
  Travel Tub™, 80
Country Cottage, 106
Cow Bells Rattle, 97
Cozi Critters™, 74
CPSC (Consumer Product Safety
  Commission), 5, 78-79, 90, 103,
  140-41
  "For Kids' Sake, Think Toy
  Safety," 141
  "Tips For Your Baby's Safety,"
  141
  "Which Toy For Which Child?,"
  141
Crackers, 38-39
Cradle, 1-2
Creative Memories, 143-44
  album supplies, 143
  photo-safe albums, 143
Creative Pegboard, 113
CRIB BIB®, 5
CribEssentials™ Mobile and
  Musical Crib Light, 90
Crib Light, 7, 90
Crib Rail Barnyard™, 91-92
Crib toys, 90-93
Cribs, 2-6
  criteria for, 5-6
  products for, 2-5
Crib sheets, 5
C-section
  pillows for, 20-21
Cubes, storage. *See* Selfix.
Cups
  snack, 75-76
  toy, 48, 112
  training, 35-36

D

Dancin' Magic, 122
Day Care Pets, 117-18
Dental care, 46-47
Diaper bags, 69-70
Diaper pails, 12
Diapers
  cloth, 10, 12
  storage of, 9, 11
Diplomat Juvenile Corp.
  Ecology Kids™ Changing
  Time™ Diaper Cover and
  Super Absorbent Diaper, 12

Rosie's Babies™ Baby Safety
    Harness, 69
Rosie's Babies™ Deluxe
    Reversible Fabric/Terry
    Cloth Fits-All Seat Cover, 74
Rosie's Babies™ Stroller
    Netting by Diplomat, 67
Super Size Toy Hammock, 58
Toy Hammock With Wall
    Hanging, 58
Discovery Cottage, 109
Discovery Music
    Bathtime Magic, 122
    Dancin' Magic, 122
    Lullaby Magic, 122
    Lullaby Magic II, 122
    Morning Magic, 122
    Simply Magic video, 122
    Traveling Magic, 122
Discovery Toys, Inc.
    Bright Builders, 112
    Giant Pegboard™, 112-13
    Gummy Yummy, 96
    Measure Up!® Cups, 112
    Place and Trace® Puzzle, 111-
        12
    Rolling Reflections, 99
    Spin, Rattle 'N' Roll™ Activity
        Rattle, 96
    TANGIBALL, 99
    Tons of Fun® Rattle, 96
    Tumble Time, 96
    What's Cookin', 114
Disney Records, Walt, 122-23
    Feel the Music, 123
    Happy to Be Here, 123
    Shakin' It, 123
Door Knob Cover With Lock
    Guard, 54
Door stop, 55
Double-Feature mirror, 14-15, 93
Dreamsheet Quick Change
    Bedding, 5
Dress-Me-Up™ Ernie, 115
Drip-less Cups, 36
Dr. Mom, 10, 135
Duet Diaper Bag, 70

E

Earth's Best, Inc.
    cereals, 37
    juices, 37

purees, 37
Easy Change, 77
Easy Feedin'™ Nighttime
    Feeder™, 30
Easy Grip® Fork and Spoon, 34
Ecology Kids™ Changing Time™
    Diaper Cover and Super
    Absorbent Diaper, 12
Eden Toys, Inc.
    Eden Music Makers, 117
    Goodnight Moon with rabbit,
        132
Enclosure, 52-53
Erewhon Apple Stroodles, 37
Erewhon Banana O's, 37
Erewhon Super O's, 37
Evenflo Juvenile Furniture Co.,
    Inc.
    Evenflo® Swing, 16
    Snack & Play® The Neat Little
        Eat Seat™, 77

F

False Bottoms garment extender,
    88
Feeding items, 33-34, 75-77. *See
    also* Mealtime.
Feeding tube device, 24
Feel the Music, 123
First Lock of Hair, 144
First Move shoe, 82
First Years/Kiddie Products Inc.
    Activity Book, 129
    Attach-A-Toy, 68
    Baby Scissors, 46
    Cabinet Safety Latch, 54
    Car Child View Mirror, 75
    Chime Rattle, 97
    Comfy-Cuff Booties, 81
    Compact Food Grinder, 76
    Drink Link™, 68
    First Keys, 96
    Fit 'N Fill Discovery Pail, 102
    Hide 'N Seek Rattle, 96-97
    My First Puzzle, 102
    My Own Toothbrush, 46
    Nightlight with Socket Cover,
        54
    Nipple Adapter, 26
    No Scratch Baby Mitts, 86
    Nursery Organizer, 11
    Soft Handled Teether Rattle, 96

Squeakie Playbook series, 129
Stack'em Up Cups, 48
Sure-Grip Suction Bowl With
   Lid, 34
Touch 'N Sound Toy TV
   Remote, 113
TumbleMates™ 4 Pack-A-Snack
   Cups, 75
Wash 'N Dry Bag, 12
Fish Eyes, 130-31
Fisher-Price®
   Activity Links Gym, 94
   Activity Walker, 100
   Baby's First Blocks, 101
   Bath Center, 40
   Big View Mirror, 92
   Bottle Organizer, 28
   Bubble Mower, 104-05
   Captain Stack, 47
   Cow Bells Rattle, 97
   Creative Pegboard, 113
   Deluxe High Chair, 32-33
   Diaper Pail, 12
   Discovery Cottage, 109
   Flow Control Cup, 35
   Gentle Glide Bassinet, 2
   Infant Dish, 76
   Kiddicraft Dress & Count
      Clown, 115
   Kiddicraft® Shape Tipper, 109
   Little People® Jetliner, 109
   Little People® School, 108-09
   Little People® School Bus, 109-
      10
   Melody Push Chime, 105
   Play Buckets, 47
   Rock-A-Stack® rings, 101
   Sand Kitchen, 116
   Sand Workshop, 116
   Soft Spray Tub, 41
   Toddler Fork & Spoon, 34
   3-in-1 Travel Tender With
      Bassinet, 80
Fit 'N Fill Discovery Pail, 102
Flap Happy, Inc.
   Flap Happy® Original Flap
      Hat, 86
Flexible Door Stops, 55
Flow Control Cup, 35
Food, baby, 37
Food grinders, 36, 76
Foods, prepared, 36-39

Footwear, 81-83
Forecees Co.
   Linky Rinks, 116-17
   Linky Rinks Creative Play
      Cards, 116
   Linky Rinks Creative Play
      Cards Kit, 116
Formula
   Accessories, 29-30
   Enfamil, 36-37
Four Dee Products
   Nurse Mate, 19
Frantz, Kittie, 18, 22, 135
Freehand® Bottle Holder, 26
Fun 'n Fruity™ Teether, 97-98
Furniture. *See* Bellini, Cabinet,
   Changing tables, Cribs, Today's
   Kids.
Funsie Onesies™, 83

G

Garden Tools, 105
Garment extender, 88
Garters, baby, 88
Gate, security, 53
Geddes Productions
   Breastfeeding Techniques That
      Work!™ videos, 22, 135
Gerber Products Company
   Circus Teethers, 97
   Collars and Snap Off Hoods,
      27
   Door Knob Cover With Lock
      Guard, 54
   Flexible Door Stops, 55
   Funsie Onesies™, 83
   Happy Elephant™ Mirror
      Rattle, 97
   Li'l Hoodl'ems™ Hooded
      Towel, 44
   Onesies® One-Piece
      Underwear, 83
   Shake 'N Spin Rattle, 97
   Spinning Teether Rattle™, 97
   3RD FOODS™ Fruit and Veggie
      Juices, 37
Gerry Baby Products Company
   Look 'N Listen Baby Monitor,
      6
   Two Years® Bath, 41
   Walk-Thru Gate, 53
Giant Pegboard™, 112-13

G'Night Wolfgang, 121
Golden Sound Story books, 128-29
Goodnight Hands, 121
Goodnight Moon, 132
Graco Children's Products
  Battery-Powered Carrier/Rocker Swing, 60
  Sport Tot-Loc® chair, 77
Graham crackers, 38
Greenwillow Books/Wm. Morrow & Co.
  Welcome, Little Baby, 133
Grinders, food, 36, 76
Grosset & Dunlap, 125
Gryphon House Early Childhood Books, 139
Guess Who I Love?, 126
Gummy Yummy, 96
Gymboree Corporation
  play program, 142
  playwear, 85
GymFinity™, 94

H

Hand in Hand, 117, 139
Hap Palmer's Follow-Along Songs, 124
Happy Baby® Deluxe Food Grinder With Tote, 36
Happy Elephant™ Mirror Rattle, 97
Happy Napper, 60
Happy to Be Here, 123
Harcourt Brace & Company
  Fish Eyes, 130-31
  Mouse Paint, 130
Harnesses, 69, 79
HarperCollins Publishers
  Childwise Catalog, 136
Hats, 86
Healthtex Bodyshirt™, 85
Healthtex, Inc.
  Bodyshirt, 85
  Playwear Denims™, 85
Health Valley Foods, Inc.
  cookies and crackers, 38
  soups, 38
Healthy Grahams Animal Cookies, 38

Healthy Times
  Baby Cream With Orchid Oil, 45
  cereals, 38
  cookies, 38-39
Heritage Album, 144
Hey, Look At Me! Baby Days, 127, 144
Hide 'N Seek Rattle, 96-97
High chairs, 31-33
Home & Roam™ Double Duty High Chair, 32
Hoods, bottle, 27
HOT + COOL BAG™, 71
HOT + COLD PAK™, 71
How to Get to Sesame Street, 128-29
How to Raise a Brighter Child, 135-36
How to Save Your Child's Life, 135
Hugga Bears cookies, 38
Hush-A-Bye Dreamsongs, 120
"Hush-A-Bye Know-How," 121

I

Infa-Dent® Finger Toothbrush and Gum Massager, 46
Infant Stim-Mobile, 14-15
INFLATE-A-POTTY, 78
Insect protection, 67-68
Island Cruiser™ Sandbox, 107
Itty Bitty Busters™, 82

J

Jesse Bear, What Will You Wear?, 131
Johnson & Johnson
  Johnson's Nursing Pads, 23
JPMA (Juvenile Products Manufacturers Association), xvii, xviii, 31, 140
  certification, 5, 52, 65, 140
  "Safe and Sound For Baby," 140
Judi's Originals
  Cozi Critters™, 74
  Dreamsheet Quick Change Bedding, 5
  Musical/Touch Lite Lamp, 6
Juices, 37

Junior Activity Gym, 106
Juvenile Products Manufacturers
Association. *See* JPMA.

K

Kangaroo Playmates™, 117
Keepers™ Clear Boxes, 56
Keepers Pop-Up Box, 57
Keepers™ Snap Cases, 56
Keepers Stacking Bins, 56
Keepers Totelocker, 57
Keepers Window Bins, 57
Keepsakes and memorabilia, 142-
44
Kiddicraft Dress & Count Clown,
115
Kiddicraft® Shape Tipper, 109
Kid Kaper® towel, 44
Kids Cubes, 58
"For Kids' Sake, Think Toy
Safety," 141
Kinder-Grip™ bottle by Playtex®,
27
K-Mart, 2, 27, 28, 32, 35, 40, 48,
62, 77, 80, 92, 94-95
Knee pads, 87

L

Lactation consultants, 18, 23
La Leche League, 18-19, 21-23
Lambskin, 3
Lamby Cuddle Rug, 3
Lamby Nursery Collection
Baby Tri-pillow, 74
Lamby Cuddle Rug, 3
Lanolin, 45
Lansinoh Laboratories
Lansinoh® for Nursing
Mothers, 23
Nature's Second Skin, 45
Latches, 53-55
Laundry bags, 11-12
Leachco
Freehand® Bottle Holder, 26
Kid Kaper® towel, 44
Ride 'N Stride, 79
Snuggle-Up™, 59, 120
Lights, 6-7
Li'l Hoodl'ems™ Hooded Towel,
44

Lillian Vernon Corp.
catalogs, 137
dinnerware set, 34
flatware fork and spoon, 34
Lilly's Kids® catalog, 137
vinyl mat, 34
Lilly's Kids® catalog, 137
Linky Rinks, 116-17
Linky Rinks Creative Play Cards,
116
Linky Rinks Creative Play Cards
Kit, 116
Listen & Learn™ Nursery Rhymes
Ball, 99-100
Little, Brown & Company, Inc.
Maisy Goes to Bed, 133
Little Engine That Could, 127
Little Miss Choo Choo, 104
Little People® Jetliner, 109
Little People® School, 108-09
Little People® School Bus, 109-10
Little Quiet Book, 132
Little Tikes Company
Airplane Teeter Totter, 106
Barnyard Crib Center, 91-92
Castle, 106-07
Country Cottage, 106
Garden Tools, 105
Island Cruiser™ Sandbox, 107
Junior Activity Gym, 106
Mini Van, 105
Play About™ House, 98
Push About™ Popper, 105
Quiet Ride™ Wagon, 105
Rocking Horse, 61
Take-a-Turn™ Puzzle, 111
Tikes Peak Road and Rail Set,
110-11
Toddle Tots® Dump Truck, 110
Toddle Tots® Noah's Ark, 48
Locks, 53-55, 57
LOVE BUG™, 67
Lullaby & Goodnight Sleepkit™,
120-21
Lullaby Berceuse, 121-22
Lullaby Magic, 122
Lullaby Magic II, 122

M

Macmillan Children's Book Group
Jesse Bear, What Will You Wear?,
131

Zoo Animals, 131
Magic Dishwasher™, 114
MagMag® Insti-Snack™ Powdered
  Formula/Snack Container, 30
MagMag Toothbrush System, 46
Maisy Goes to Bed, 133
Marran International
  Baby Bumpers® knee pads, 87
Marshall Baby Products
  Advanced MagMag™ Training
    Cup System, 35
  Happy Baby® Deluxe Food
    Grinder With Tote, 36
  MagMag® Insti-Snack™
    Powdered Formula/Snack
    Container, 30
  MagMag Toothbrush System,
    46
Mats
  bath, 42
  napping, 60
  playing, 59-60
Maya Group
  Powdered Milk Container, 30
MCA Records
  Baby Beluga, 123-24
Mead Johnson Nutritionals
  Enfamil, 36-37
Mealtime
  bottles, 27
  cups, 35-36
  feeding items, 33-34
  food, 36-39
  formula, 36-37
  juices, 37
  preparation, 36, 39
  prepared foods, 36-39
Measure Up!® Cups, 112
Medela, 20-22, 24
  Classic™ Breastpump, 21-22
  Manual Breastpump, 20-21
  Supplemental Nursing
    System™ (SNS), 22, 24
  Universal Pumping System
    accessory kit, 21
Melody Push Chime, 105
Merrybooks & More
  Hey, Look At Me! Baby Days,
    127, 144
Mestman, Sadie, 46-47
Meyerhoff, Michael, 90
Microwavable, 34

Microwave Warm 'n Serve™ Dish,
  34
Mini Van, 105
Mirrors, 14-15, 75, 92-93, 99
Mitts, 86
Mobiles, 13-15, 90-91
Monitor. *See* Baby monitors.
Morning Magic, 122
Mouse Paint, 130
*Mr. Rogers First Experience Books:
  Going to the Dentist*, 47
Music For Little People, 121-24,
  138
  G'Night Wolfgang, 121
  Lullaby Berceuse, 121-22
Musical Lullaby and Goodnight
  Book, 133
Musical Shape & Sort™, 101-02
Musical/Touch Lite Lamp, 6
My First Buster™, 82
My First Puzzle, 102
My Quiet Book, 114-15
My Potty Game, 43

N

NAP® Nipple and Pacifier
  Sanitizing Device, 28
National Highway Traffic Safety
  Administration (NHTSA), 73,
  141
"Child Safety Seat Recall"
  package, 141
National Parenting Center, The,
  xviii, 42, 141-42
  awards program, 142
  ParentTalk, 142
Nature's Second Skin, 45
Netting, stroller, 67
New Age Concepts
  Soothe 'n Snooze Bassinet, 2
New American Library
  Dr. Mom, 10, 135
Newborne Co.
  Sinkadink, the Kid's Sink, 42
NewDay's Choice Baby Wipes, 11
NHTSA. *See* National Highway
  Traffic Safety Administration.
Night light, 7, 54, 90
Nipples, 25-26
  silicone, 25-26
Noah's Ark. *See* Little Tikes.

North States Industries, Inc.
  Superyard, 52
Numbers, 126
Nurse Mate nursing pillow, 19
Nursery products, 1-13
Nursing, 18-24
Nursing pads, 23
Nu-Tec Health Products
  Infa-Dent® Finger Toothbrush
  and Gum Massager, 46

O

OFNA Baby Products
  Toddler Shield, 51
Once Upon a Potty book/video, 131
One Green Frog, 125-26
Onesies® One-Piece Underwear, 83
One Step Ahead™, 5, 23, 26, 32, 44, 46, 53, 59, 60, 78-79, 137-38
1-2-3 Bike, 108
Only Natural, Inc.
  Babycakes®, 44
  Camomile soap, 44
Oppenheim Toy Portfolio, xviii, 136-37
  awards, 15, 95, 137
  publication, 136
Organizational systems, 9, 55-56, 64
Organizers. *See also* Bins, Boxes.
  bottle, 28-29
  changing table, 11-12
  closet, 58
  drawer, 9
  food, 36
  storage, 55-58
  toy, 57-58
ORGANIZER™ by Prince
  Lionheart, 11
OshKosh B'Gosh, Inc., 83-85
  Bib Overall, 83
  Busy Body Bib Overalls, 84
  Busy Body Shortalls, 84
  Traditional Bib Overall, 84
  Traditional Shortall, 84
Over in the Meadow, 129

P

Padders® soft bootie/shoes, 81

Pansy Ellen
  CribEssentials™ Mobile and
  Musical Crib Light, 90-91
  Crib Light, 7
Pansy Ellen Bright Starts™
  Crib Mirror, 93
Parachute Express. *See* Disney Records.
Parenting books, 134-37
Parents' Choice, 136
Parents' Choice Awards, xviii, 13, 92, 94-95, 99, 108, 114, 116, 120-23, 136
Parents Magazine Child
  Development Toys. *See* Child
  Development Toys.
ParentTalk, 142
Pat the Bunny, 127-28
Pattern-Pals, 14
Pattern-Play, 14
Pearcy Company
  Bottle Dryer, 28-29
Peg Perego U.S.A., Inc.
  Amico, 66
  Deluxe High Chair, 31
  High Chair/Youth Chair, 31-32
  Tender tandem stroller, 66
Perfectly Safe® Catalog, 42, 51-53, 88, 138
Perfectly Safe® Home, 41, 51, 136
Personal care products, 44
Photo albums, 142-44
Photo Organizer Storage Kit, 144
Pillows
  back support, 20
  breastfeeding, 19-20
  pregnancy, 20
  sitting and playing, 59-60
  travel, 74-75
Place and Trace® Puzzle, 111-12
Play About™ House, 98
Play Buckets, 47
Play gym, 94-95
Playskool®
  Animals, 115
  Baby Safe-Store Pail™, 55
  Baby Stroller Tray, 68
  Busy Bubble Maker™, 49
  Busy Camera, 98-99
  Busy Guitar, 99
  Busy Splash 'n Play™, 49
  Click 'N Swirl Rattle, 97

Dinosaurs, 115
Dress-Me-Up™ Ernie, 115
Easy Feedin'™ Nighttime
  Feeder™, 30
Easy Grip® Fork and Spoon,
  34
Fun 'n Fruity™ Teether, 97-98
Horses, 115
Letter Wood Blocks, 113
Microwave Warm 'n Serve™
  Dish, 34
1-2-3 Bike™, 108
Pur® Silicone Nipples, 26
Sand Works™, 115-16
Sesame Street Babies, 115
Sesame Street Hand Puppets,
  115
Scooper® Bowl, 33
Scooper® Plate, 33
Soft Scoop Spoon™, 34
Touch'ems™ Sesame Street
Pals, 115
Play Table, 61
Playtex®
  Cherubs Collection Training
    Cup, 35
  Kinder-Grip™ bottle, 27
Play yard, 52-53
Pockets of Learning
  ABC Carrybag, 114
  ABC Wallhanging, 108
  Musical Lullaby and Goodnight
    Book, 133
  My Quiet Book, 114-15
Poke & Look books, 125-26
Polliwog™ Bathtub Sidewall
  Cushion, 41
POPUPS™ Expandable Nursers,
  76
Potty, Century 4-Way, 42-43
Potty Training Your Baby, 43, 137
Pour & Store Formula Caps, 29
Powdered Milk Container, 30
Pregnancy Wedge, 20
Prepared foods, 36-39
Price, xviii, xx, xxi
Prince Lionheart, xix
  HOT + COOL BAG™, 71
  HOT + COLD PAK™, 71
  LOVE BUG™, 67
  NAP® Nipple and Pacifier
    Sanitizing Device, 28

POPUPS™ Expandable
  Nursers, 76
SANI-STOR™, 28
SLIP-NOT MAT, 42
STROLLER ACCESSORY BAR,
  68
STROLLER SHIELD, 68
UFO Stages, 36
UFO, Universal Food
  Organizer, 36
Pudgy Board Books, 126
Pumps, breast, 20-22
Pur® Silicone Nipples, 26
Push About™ Popper, 105
Putnam & Grosset Group
  Baby's Peek-A-Boo Album, 126-
    27
  Guess Who I Love?, 126
  Little Engine That Could, 127
  Mr. Rogers...Going to the Dentist,
    47
  One Green Frog, 125-26
  Spot's First Words, 126
  What Does Baby See?, 126
  Wheels Go Round, 126
  Wheels on the Bus, 126
  Who Says Quack?, 126
Puzzles, 102, 109, 111-12

Q
Quiet Ride™ Wagon, 105
Quilt, 16-17, 59

R
Raffi. See MCA Records.
Random House, Inc.
  Baby Animals, 131-32
  Baby's ABC, 132
  Baby's First Picture Book, 131-32
  Little Quiet Book, 132
Recalls, xviii, 141
Red Calliope Comforter, 17
Ricklen, Neil, 130, back cover
  photo
Ride 'N Stride, 79
Ride-on toys, 61, 104-06, 108
Right Start Catalog, 5, 26, 32, 33,
  46, 53, 58-59, 63, 78, 87, 138
Roaring Choo Choo, 104
Roaring Fire Engine™, 104

Rock-A-Bye Baby
Baby's First Year, 13-14, 144
Baby-Snuggleheads, 3-4
Basic EasyDry® Baby Towel, 43
Bath, Bed'n'Beach Reversible, Hooded Robe, 44
CARTA-KID, 79
Classic EasyDry® Baby Towel, 43
Classic FancyDry® Hooded Towel, 43
Comfy Wipe Warmer, 10
My Potty Game, 43
Rock-A-Bye Bear®, 3-4
Rock-A-Bye Bunny®, 4
Rock-A-Bye Collection, Volume One, 120
Rock-A-Bye Collection, Volume Two, 120
Rock-A-Stack® rings, 101
Rocker, 61
Rocking chair accessories, 62
Rocking horse, 61
Rock-R-Roll™, 62
Rock-R-Roll With Pockets, 62
Rolling Reflections, 99
Rosie's Babies™ Baby Safety Harness, 69
Rosie's Babies™ Deluxe Reversible Fabric/Terry Cloth Fits-All Seat Cover, 74
Rosie's Babies™ Stroller Netting by Diplomat, 67
Rubbermaid Inc.
Cart Wheels™ Bin Cart, 57
Keepers™ Clear Boxes, 56
Keepers™ Pop-Up Box, 57
Keepers™ Snap Cases, 56
Keepers™ Stacking Bins, 56
Keepers™ Totelocker, 57
Keepers™ Window Bins, 57
Servin' Saver™ containers, 34
Ruggie Bear® Activity Play Mat, 17

S

"Safe and Sound For Baby," 140
Safe Care Products, Inc.
Polliwog™ Bathtub Sidewall Cushion, 41
Safety, 50-55, 71-74, 89, 135, 140-
41
Safety 1st
Baby Cassette Teether, 97
Baby's Own Laundry Bag, 12
Bath Pal, 42
Cabinet Slide Lock, 54
Car-Go Bag, 75
Lil' Muncher Snack Box, 75
N'ICE BEAR, 63
Oven Lock, 54
Parent's Helper Rearview Magnifier, 75
Pour & Store Formula Caps, 29
Small Object Tester, 55, 108
Swivel Bath Seat, 42
Toilet Seat Covers, 78
Wash'r Dry Bag, 12
SafetyBelt Safe U.S.A., 71-74, 141
Sandbox Industries
BUMP AROUND™, 8-9
CRIB BIB®, 5
Rock-R-Roll™, 62
Rock-R-Roll With Pockets, 62
Sandbox Sandbag, 71
Stroller Cover, 69
Sand Kitchen, 116
Sand Works™, 115-16
Sand Workshop, 116
SANI-STOR™, 28
Scissors, baby, 46
Scooper® Bowl, 33
Scooper® Plate, 33
Sea Shell™ Rattle, 97
Security gate, 53
Seating, indoor, 58-62
Selfix, Inc.
Cubby Cubes, 58
Kids Cubes, 58
Sesame Street, 115, 125, 128
Sesame Street Babies, 115
Sesame Street Hand Puppets, 115
Shake 'N Spin Rattle, 97
Shakin' It, 123
Shampoo, baby, 45
Sheets, 5, 63
Ship Shape Village, 48
Shirt Anchors, 87
Shoes, 81-83
Shortall, 84
Sigh of Relief, 135
Simon & Schuster, 129-30
Baby's Colors, 130

How to Raise a Brighter Child,
    135-36
Little Book of Numbers, 130
Over in the Meadow, 129
Perfectly Safe® Home, 41, 51,
    136
What's Inside?, 129-30
Simply Magic video, 122
Sinkadink, the Kid's Sink, 42
Skincare products, 45-46
Sleeper Keeper™, 63
SLIP-NOT MAT, 42
Small Object Tester, 55, 108
Smile Tote Inc.
    änsa® Sipper, 76
    Toddler Traveling Juice Cup,
        77
    Toddler Tumbler, 77
Snap & Go® Bottle Rings, 69
SNS, 24
Snuggle-Up™, 59, 120
Soap, 44-45
Soft Handled Teether Rattle, 96
Soft Scoop Spoon™, 34
Someday Baby, Inc/J. Aaron
    Brown
    Child's Gift of Lullabies®, 120
    *Rock-A-Bye Collection, Volume
        One*, 120
    *Rock-A-Bye Collection, Volume
        Two*, 120
    Snuggle-Up™, 59, 120
Soothe 'n Snooze Bassinet, 2
Soups, canned, 38
Spin, Rattle 'N' Roll™ Activity
    Rattle, 96
Spinning Teether Rattle™, 97
Spot Board Books, Little, 126
Spot's First Words, 126
Squeakie Playbook series, 129
Stardreamer, 122
Storage organizers, 55-58
Stride Rite Children's Group, Inc.
    Baby Tech™, 82
    First Move, 82
STROLLER ACCESSORY BAR, 68
Stroller Cover, 69
Strollers, 64-69
    accessories for, 67-69
    features, 64-66
    recommended, 65-67
    types, 64-65

STROLLER SHIELD, 68
Stroller Umbrella, 69
Summer Infant Products
    Summer Playtime Soft Seat™,
        15-16
Sunglasses, 86
Sun protection, 69, 86
Super Chubby Lift-Flap Board
    Books, 130
Super Size Toy Hammock, 58
Superyard, 52
Supplemental Nursing System, 21,
    24
Swings, 16, 60

T
Tabor Crib-n-Twin, 6
Tag-Along Stroll-A-Bag, 66, 69
Take-a-Turn™ Puzzle, 111
TANGIBALL, 99
Tapes, audio, 119-24
Target Stores, 2, 12, 16, 27, 28, 32,
    35, 40, 48, 58, 62, 77, 80, 92,
    94-95, 104-05, 107, 117
Teethers and small activity toys,
    96-98
Tellalian, Louise, 22
Tender Moments
    Bottle Burper®, 26
Tender tandem stroller, 66
Texas Instruments
    Listen & Learn™ Nursery
        Rhymes Ball, 99-100
    Musical Shape & Sort™, 101-
        02
Thermos. *See* Zojirushi Airpot.
Thermometers
    bath, 42
    ear, 62
Thermoscan, 62-63
3RD FOODS™ Fruit and Veggie
    Juices, 37
Tikes Peak Road and Rail Set,
    110-11
Times to Treasure
    Goodnight Hands, 121
    Hush-A-Bye Dreamsongs, 120
    "*Hush-A-Bye Know-How*," 121
    Lullaby & Goodnight
        Sleepkit™, 120-21
"Tips For Your Baby's Safety," 141
TNPC. *See* National Parenting

Center.
Today's Kids, Inc.
    Activity Rocker™, 61
    All Star Basketball®, 107
    Alpha Desk™, 61
    GymFinity™, 94
    Magic Dishwasher™, 114
    Play Table, 61
Toddle Tots® Dump Truck, 110
Toddle Tots® Noah's Ark, 48
Toddler bed, 6
Toddler Fork & Spoon, 34
Toddler Shield, 51
Toddle Tots® School Bus, 110
Toddler Traveling Juice Cup, 77
Toddler Tumbler, 77
Toilet Seat Covers, 78
Toilet training. *See* Potty.
Tombrello, Stephanie, 74
Tom's of Maine
    Natural Baby Shampoo, 45
    Natural Toothpaste for
        Children, 47
Tons of Fun® Rattle, 96
Toothbrushes, 46-47
Toothpaste, 47
Tote bags, 11-12, 70-71
Tot-Loc® chair, 77
Tot Tenders
    Tot Tenders Baby Carrier, 7-8
    Tot Tether, 79
Tot Tether, 79
Totelocker Jr., 57
Touch'ems™ Sesame Street Pals,
    115
Toy Hammock With Wall
    Hanging, 58
Toys. *See also* Mirrors, Mobiles.
    accessory for attaching, 68
    for babies, 89-102
    bath, 47-49
    cloth, 114-15, 117-18
    crib, 90-93
    criteria for selecting, 89-90, 95-
        96
    fine motor, 103, 108-14
    first, 93-95
    gross motor, 99, 102, 103-08
    from nine months, 101
    organizers for, 57-58
    play value of, 90
    push, 100, 104-05

realistic, 104, 113-114
ride-on, 61, 104-06, 108
sand, 47, 71, 115-16
from six months, 98
sorter, 101-102
special needs, 137
teethers and small activity toys,
    96-98
for toddlers, 103-18
traveling, 103, 114-18
Toys R Us, 2, 12, 16, 27, 28, 32,
    35, 36, 40, 47, 58, 62, 77-78, 80,
    92, 94-95, 100, 104-5, 107
Towels, 43-44
Tracking Tube, 93-93
Travel
    changing time and, 77-78
    checklists, 64
    mealtime accessories, 75-77
    overnight, 70, 80
    toys, 103, 114-18
Travel Tender, 80
Travel Tub™, 80
Traveling Magic, 122
Tricycle, 108
Tuffy Tiny Books, 126
Tuffy Tote Books, 126
Tumble Time, 96
TV Remote toy, 113-14

U
UFO, Universal Food Organizer,
    36
Uncle Randy's Baby Garters, 88
University Products, 144
    acid-free boxes, supplies, 144
    photo albums, storage, 144
Un-Petroleum Jelly®, 45
U.S. Consumer Product Safety
    Commission. *See* CPSC.
U.S. Mills, Inc.
    Erewhon Apple Stroodles, 37
    Erewhon Banana O's, 37
    Erewhon Super O's, 37

V
Varga, Jim, 13
VCR lock, 53
Victor's Latch, 53
Video Halt, 53
Videos

breastfeeding, 22
music, 122, 124

W

Walkers, 100
Wal-Mart, 2, 12, 16, 27, 28, 32, 35,
40, 48, 77, 80, 92, 94, 105
Welcome, Little Baby, 133
Western Publishing Company, Inc.
*Hap Palmer's Follow-Along
Songs,* 124
How to Get to Sesame Street,
128-29
Pat the Bunny, 127-28
What Does Baby See?, 126
What to Eat When You're Expecting,
134-35
What to Expect the First Year, 25,
134-35
*What to Expect While You're
Expecting,* 134-35
What's Cookin', 114
What's Inside?, 129-30
Wheels Go Round, 126
Wheels on the Bus, 126
"Which Toy For Which Child?,"
141
Who Says Quack?, 126
Wimmer-Ferguson
Double-Feature mirror, 14-15,
93
Infant Stim-Mobile, 14-15
Pattern-Pals, 14-15
Pattern-Play, 14
"What Does Baby See?," 136
Wimmer-Ferguson Double-Feature
Mirror, 14, 15, 93
Wipes. *See* Baby wipes.
Womanly Art of Breastfeeding, 23
Womb-like environment, 1-5
Workman Publishing
Baby Let's Eat!, 39, 136
*What to Eat When You're
Expecting,* 134-35
What to Expect the First Year,
25, 134-35
*What to Expect While You're
Expecting,* 134-35

X

Xenon Entertainment Group
How to Save Your Child's Life,
135

Z

Zojirushi Airpots, 9-10
Zoo Animals, 131

Shopping Notes

You can use this page and the following pages to keep your own shopping and product information organized in one place. Be sure to date all phone calls or shopping trips and write down the names of all people with whom you talk.